THE THEATER ARTS
AND
THE TEACHING
OF SECOND LANGUAGES

STEPHEN M. SMITH

ADDISON-WESLEY PUBLISHING COMPANY
Reading, Massachusetts
Menlo Park, California • Don Mills, Ontario
Amsterdam • London • Manila • Singapore • Sydney • Tokyo

THE ADDISON-WESLEY SECOND LANGUAGE PROFESSIONAL LIBRARY SERIES

Sandra J. Savignon
Consulting Editor

HIGGINS, John and JOHNS, Tim
Computers in Language Learning

SAVIGNON, Sandra J. and
BERNS, Margie S.
Initiatives in Communicative Language Teaching

SAVIGNON, Sandra J.
Communicative Competence: Theory and Classroom Practice

VENTRIGLIA, Linda
Conversations of Miguel and Maria

WALLERSTEIN, Nina
Language and Culture in Conflict

Photos by Susan C. Jenkins.

Library of Congress Cataloging in Publication Data

Smith, Stephen M., 1955–
  The theater arts and the teaching of second languages.

  (Second language professional library)
  Bibliography: p.
  Includes index.
  1. Language and languages—Study and teaching. 2. Drama in education.
I. Title. II. Title: Theater arts and the teaching of second languages. III. Series.
P53.S57 1984   418'.007'1   83-21524
ISBN 0-201-07163-0

ISBN: 0-201-07163-0
ABCDEFGHIJKL-AL-8987654

Player: Uncertainty is the normal state. You're nobody special.

Guildenstern: But for God's sake what are we supposed to do?!

Player: Relax. Respond. That's what people do. You can't go through life questioning your situation at every turn.

Guildenstern: But we don't know what's going on, or what to do with ourselves. We don't know how to *act*.

From: *Rosencrantz and Guildenstern Are Dead*, by Tom Stoppard

For my parents and my wife

Preface

Here is a book for language teachers who wish to know about the usefulness of theater arts for language teaching. This book is both practical and theoretical, containing exercises and techniques as well as fundamental theory. It is for all language teachers, but especially for teachers of adults and adolescents who are at intermediate and advanced levels of second or foreign language proficiency, and who are in all types of learning situations: universities, intensive programs, evening programs, elementary and secondary schools, and other language learning groups. Teachers of beginners and young children will also recognize the relevance of this book and its exercises to their students.

It is not surprising that many language teachers have seen the value of looking to the theater arts for language teaching techniques. When speaking of actors' training, it is natural to speak of language learning and teaching. Actors use language as the main tool of their craft, and they have been in the business of solving language learning problems for a long time. They have developed techniques for expanding their range of expression, both verbal and non-verbal. Each role an actor plays requires a unique accent, unique vocabulary, unique gestures, and a unique cultural background. To learn new roles the actor must break old habits, and acquire new ones. Frequently switching roles, the actor must be flexible and sensitive to human nature. The actor must observe the different ways in which people speak, move, and communicate.

Although many of the techniques used by today's theater artists are descended from practices of centuries past, it would not be accurate to regard them as "old fashioned" techniques since today's artist uses them in a contemporary manner. In the theater world, respect for tradition, experience, and disciplined training is balanced by respect for innovation, individuality, and creativity. Times change, and artists and their art must be adaptable.

There is a similar forward-looking mentality that characterizes the state of the art of modern day language teaching. Trying not to forget the lessons of the past, we are constantly striving to develop new and better techniques for language teaching. Like the theater artist, we sometimes reach for the "different" simply because it is different, in order to see if it will develop into something that is better.

This book is intended to provide ideas that will expand your repertoire of language teaching techniques, ideas that you will be able to *adapt* to your own, very personal teaching style. You will recognize some fundamental language teaching concepts presented here. Other ideas will be new to you. Your task is to extend the ideas, whether they are familiar to you or not, to create something both different and better for your own teaching.

The theater arts can be introduced into the language teaching curriculum in varying amounts: either as part of a teacher's general philosophy, or as supplementary materials, or as a full-blown theater production course in which language learners perform plays in the second language. Languages cannot, however, be taught through theater techniques alone. Elements of the theater arts must be integrated into programs containing other forms of instruction and opportunities to experience the language. It is the responsibility of the qualified teacher to decide when, and in what quantities, to apply particular teaching methods or techniques, to any given group.

The first two chapters of this book are designed to give teachers the *theoretical* background necessary to make the most out of the *practical* applications in Chapters 3 and 4.

Chapter 1 is a discussion of the fundamental relationship between the theater arts and language teaching. Chapter 2 examines how language is taught in the drama rehearsal. Chapter 3 provides a range of practical applications in the form of individual exercises for integration into your own language teaching syllabus. Chapter 4, also practical, describes the process of play production leading to performance so that you, acting as a theatrical director, can give students an intensive and rewarding language experience by leading them through the play production process. Through the experience of play production, both teachers and students will make discoveries about language and communication, and most importantly, they will make discoveries about themselves as communicators.

You will see that the theater arts has something for all language teachers. Although play production and performance are naturally not for everyone, the concepts and approaches theater shares with language teaching are useful for all language teachers—even within the constraints of the most rigid programs—and it is doubtful that one could be a good language teacher without an understanding of them.

Acknowledgments

I wish to extend sincere appreciation to Sandra Savignon for inviting me to write this book, and for her critical review of the manuscript and subsequent suggestions. A special debt of gratitude must also go to H. Douglas Brown for encouraging me to develop, practice, and write about these ideas. Both of these people have made valuable contributions to language teaching as a creative profession, and I am grateful to be one of the many teachers who have been influenced by their work.

Enthusiasm is contagious and I am, therefore, also indebted to those actors, directors, teachers of language and the performing arts, and members of my language-learning theater groups who have inspired me with their energy and creativity.

A special thanks goes out to Byron Bush and the people at Addison-Wesley for their hours of work in preparing the manuscript for production.

Contents

Chapter **4** **Play Production for Language Learning Groups:**   128
            How to Organize and Direct Your Own Theater
            Group

Chapter 1

Common Principles: Parallels Between the Theater Arts and Language Learning and Teaching

The more exposure one has to language teaching and the theater arts, the more aware one becomes of the many parallels that exist between the two domains. Many of the concepts associated with the teaching of foreign languages are also fundamental concepts of the theater. This chapter addresses these and other parallels, giving a theoretical background that demonstrates how it is that theater theory maps so neatly onto language teaching and learning theory. It also will become evident, as you read, that the theater arts do indeed have much to offer the language teacher.

Actors learn about how people communicate as they search for ways to communicate the message of the play to the audience. Hodge (1971) states:

> What we are not usually so aware of is how actors continually assault our senses by making us constantly taste, smell, and touch, as well as see and hear. We are inclined to take them for granted because much of what a good actor does is usually so deftly and subtly done and is so right and truthful that we are rarely conscious of the process.

The "good actor" that Hodge is talking about must have a good understanding of how the complex network of very subtle details "communicates" messages. In daily life, these details are at work communicating. Although one intuitively picks up messages from them, one does not necessarily understand how it is that they are communicating. Actors and language learners clearly have a need to learn to understand and even manipulate the most subtle aspects of communication.

GOALS, OBSTACLES, AND STRATEGIES

What are some of the parallels between language teaching and theater? Most fundamentally, actors and language learners share common *goals*, the most important being effective "performance," that is, communicating the intended, appropriate message. In order to communicate, actors, like language learners, have to be able to do three things:

1. They have to be able to decide what they want to communicate, i.e., what is appropriate for the given situation?
2. They must then decide how to communicate that message.
3. Finally they must have the flexibility to implement their decisions, or in other words, they must be able to *perform with competence*. This is perhaps the most difficult task of all.

Actors and language learners also share common *obstacles* in learning to convey meaning. They must learn to deal with new language and new roles, to understand their own inhibitions and confounding habits, and to develop the ability to control their own instruments, that is, their bodies, their voices, and their minds.

It stands to reason that actors and language learners can make use of the same *strategies* in overcoming the *obstacles* that stand in the way of effective communication.

Many language learning and teaching strategies are blended into the theatrical rehearsal process. This is not unusual since actors must be students of language. It is interesting that many of the language teaching strategies that have been inherent in the theater process for centuries have only become widely popularized in language teaching over the past two decades. This has occurred as language teaching has moved away from structural linguistics-oriented approaches and into areas suggested by sociolinguistics and humanistic psychology. We can safely say that elements of modern day language teaching methodology have been part of the theater process for hundreds of years, even if we look back only as far as the Italian *Commedia dell'arte* theater of the Renaissance. The "Commedia" was a theatrical style in which actors entertained audiences through exaggerated performances of basic human roles: heroes, villains, lovers, enemies, royalty, servants, merchants, clergymen, wisemen, and fools. Performers of the Commedia sought an optimum integration of verbal and nonverbal language. So as to adapt themselves to play any role their performance situation demanded, the actors cultivated their instruments—their voices for speaking and singing, and their bodies for tumbling, sword fighting, and eloquent movement. A command of elocution and proper deportment and a knowledge of language and human behavior were required of the actors of the day.

Today, the study of language remains the main task of the actor. It is not enough for the actor to speak only his or her own language. The actor must learn a new language with each new role! This includes, of course, learning about the behavior and mentality of the individual character as well as the culture from which he or she comes.

Note, for example, the range of English usage in the few examples below. It is safe to say that no actor uses all of these language types in daily life. A linguistic and cultural analysis of these characters must take place before the actor can begin to act.

1. O Romeo, Romeo! Wherefore art thou Romeo?
   Deny thy father, and refuse thy name;
   Or, if thou wilt not, be but sworn my love,
   And I'll no longer be a Capulet.

   [Wm. Shakespeare, *Romeo and Juliet*]

2. *Kathy*: Ruthie, I'm telling you, he's serious. You know what he told me? He thinks the whole anti-war movement is a goddamn farce. That's what he said. I mean, shit, I really thought we were relating on that one. It's not like I'm asking the guy to go burn himself or anything. It's just, I mean, he knows how I feel about this war and he's just doing it to be shitty. I know what it is. He's like, reaching out, trying to relate to me on a personal level. Oh! Ruth, it's all too much. He went to a cowboy film.

   [Michael Weller, *Moonchildren*]

3. *Constable*: Your Worship. I'm asking you formal. You've got agitators here, and they won't stop at throwing stones: that's frank.

   Mayor: (angrily) I said not yet. We'll try it my road first. Godsake, man, what's four soldiers agen the lot of 'em? This town's wintered up, you'll get no more help till there's a thaw. So work on that.

   [John Arden, *Sergeant Musgrave's Dance*]

4. *Carlyle*: And everybody just takes it. It ain't our war brother. I'm tellin' you. That's what gets me. It ain't our war no how because it ain't our country and that's what burns my ass. That and everybody just sittin' and takin' it. They gonna be . . . kickin' and stompin'— everybody here maybe one week from shippin' out to get blown clean away, and man, whata they doin'? They doin' what they told.

   [David Rabe, *Streamers*]

Before the native English speaking actress can deliver good Shakespearean English (Example 1) she must spend some time learning the language, not only what it means (wherefore = why, etc.) but how it is spoken, e.g., intonation, pronunciation, and so forth.

The same actress may find herself playing Kathy or Ruthie (Example 2) as well as Juliet (Example 1). Kathy and Ruthie are American college women living in a house with American college men in the late sixties, experimenting with sex and drugs, and protesting against the war in Vietnam. In this excerpt, Kathy is telling Ruthie about her boyfriend, Bob, who has just received his notice to report for his induction physical. Much to their horror, he is going to go; they are disappointed that he is not going to burn his draft card. Kathy and Ruthie are nearly the same age as Juliet, and, like Juliet, they speak "English," but not the same English.

In Example 3, the Constable and Mayor use yet a different variety of English. They are officials of a small coal mining town in Yorkshire, England at the turn of the century. In Example 4, the actor finds yet another variety of English. Carlyle is a black American, raised in a ghetto, who is about to be shipped off to fight in Vietnam. He is living in the same country, at the same time as Kathy and Ruthie, and is talking about the same war. He is also the same age as Kathy and Ruthie, but he speaks a "different" language.

Actors, clearly, are students of language. Their study of language means, of course, more than a discrete-point analysis of structure or phonology. It means the study of language as a living network of interacting variables, sometimes abstract, and always integrated. Since the art of acting involves so much language learning, language learners can benefit from being students of acting. But it is not only the learner who can look to theater for a counterpart. The role of the language teacher is similar to the role of the theatrical director—to create a setting conducive to language learning, and to direct the learners toward the attainment of their goal, that of effective communication.

In order to become skilled at interacting spontaneously in the second language, language learners need the opportunity to practice language without inhibition and without interruption from the teacher. However, learners also need to receive correction and explanation from the teacher. A strength of the drama rehearsal as a pedagogical instrument is that it provides both the freedom and the motivation for learners to develop skill in spontaneous communication, and it is also a forum in which the teacher/director is able to intervene frequently as an instructor. The actors and director can focus on discrete elements of language, but spontaneity and freedom are also inherent in the process, allowing for individual learner differences and allowing actors to be exposed to language that is authentic.

If we look closely at the drama rehearsal and what is being investigated and learned, we come up with a most attractive list of elements that we all would like to have in our language classes. I hesitate to begin listing these elements at the risk of giving the impression that a discrete-point analysis is appropriate, when what I really intend to express is that theater's contribution to language teaching is greater than that, just as language itself is greater than the most exhaustive listing of discrete points.

Nonetheless, for pragmatic reasons, I will attempt to list what is being taught. In the drama rehearsal, we have a language class that teaches: grammar; language functions; culture; pronunciation and intonation; language "coping" strategies like circumlocution and paraphrasing; role playing; appreciation of underlying meaning, that is, how to analyze individuals and situations using available linguistic and extra-linguistic data; appreciation of non-verbal communication; interpretation of subtext, that is, reading between the lines; using the script as literature and analyzing it as a chunk of discourse; observation skills; communication, i.e., self-expression; empathy; exploitation of the memory, including kinesthetic memory, tonal memory, and sense memory; sensitivity to speech dynamics like tempo and rhythm; self-confidence in using the "second" language; and lexical, physical, and emotional vocabulary.

Motivation is a good word to summarize what drama gives us. All of these language elements are incorporated into one event, the drama rehearsal. In a drama rehearsal, learners are highly motivated to work purposefully not only on authentic language, but also on many different, isolated language problems. In contrast, in many conventional language classes, students, not feeling the need to conquer particular problems at a given moment, may simply respond to a teacher's prompting with a "Why should I?" attitude. Students learn best that which they feel they have a need to learn. There is no substitute for motivation.

DEVELOPING COMMUNICATION SKILLS: THE GROUP

Clearly, language teachers and play directors are faced with handling many of the same sensitive aspects of human dynamics. Built into the theater process is a means of coping with these human elements. The following sections of this chapter elaborate on this similarity by discussing aspects of the drama rehearsal that may be successfully incorporated into classroom teaching.

Inhibition

Ego and self-esteem are on the line in the foreign language classroom much as they are in the emotion-charged atmosphere of the drama rehearsal. Language is a very personal matter—an expression of self. When our ability to express ourselves is reduced, as it is when we use a second language, we risk our psychological well-being every time we try to speak. The director and the language teacher are in a position to preserve or damage the exposed egos of the actors and language learners. In rehearsal, actors are called upon to sum up and then bare a variety of real emotions. They must get rid of inhibitions that protect the fragile human ego and be willing to go out on an emotional limb, take chances, be wrong, look silly, then try again. Inhibitions are systematically reduced in rehearsals until the emotional valves are open and the honest emotions of the role are flowing. Actors' self-esteem must be preserved in order to facilitate continued honesty, openness, and flexibility in rehearsal. The director must work with actors to break down defenses that prevent them from being empathic, for empathy is a key to understanding the character to be portrayed as a real, living, feeling human being. Note the parallel with the cross-cultural experience of newcomers to a foreign culture. Empathy—putting oneself "in another's shoes"—can help one's understanding of culture.

The Ensemble

The best plays are created by a "tight ensemble." This means that the actors know each other *well*, and that they trust each other. They seek advice from one another and ask for feedback. They do not fear making "mistakes" in rehearsals. That's what rehearsals are for. The same situation is beneficial to a group of language learners. They should feel free to criticize one another in a constructive manner, and they should learn to enjoy experimenting with the new language in front of their peers.

Language teachers can foster this feeling by minimizing the inhibitions of their students. The most obvious approach is to avoid making students' inhibitions any worse than they already are. The language class, like the rehearsal, should be an atmosphere conducive to open experimentation with the second language. It is much easier to be open and relaxed in front of friends than strangers.

In order to begin creating an ensemble, however, a teacher must first gain the trust of the students. Often, at the beginning of a course, it is best to avoid bombarding learners with too much overt "theater" technique, which they may not regard as language teaching. Sometimes it is good trust-building strategy to begin a course with enough "conventional" language teaching so that the students feel that they are, indeed, in a language class. Once a mutual respect has been established in the classroom, students are more likely to be productive using "new" techniques.

To create the ensemble atmosphere, early class activities should emphasize students' names, personalities, and backgrounds. Outside of class, meetings in a local pub or cafe, coffee hours, pot-luck dinners, parties, and any group activity provide extra, relaxing opportunities to practice language in social settings. They can be crucial to the development of an ensemble. The teacher, like the director, must be ready to take time to shape a class into a good working ensemble.

Games

Games are frequently used in drama rehearsal to tighten the ensemble. One of the main obstacles for actors, and language learners, to overcome is the "adult" reaction to expressing oneself truthfully. Dignity is at a premium in the adult world. Feelings and emotions are suppressed. Games, used wisely, can help adults rediscover the freedom they knew as children. Games "allow" the adults to "play" in front of their peers. Through games, ensemble members become acquainted. The ensemble begins to operate as a unit. Its members begin to trust and cooperate.

There are books available that are full of language-teaching games. However, almost any game could be considered a language game. For the purpose of ensemble building, nearly any game that the students can play will do. Inter-class competitions are particularly rewarding. In addition to increasing the chances that the students will get to know students outside their own class, thereby increasing their second-language speaking–social circle, the competing students develop a feeling of "belonging" to their own group. Their classmates become teammates, working together to achieve a common goal. Trivia contests, charades, and guessing games, to name but a few, are ideal for ensemble building.

Rehearsals often begin with a game or two in order to *warm up* the ensemble. Actors always warm up individually or as a group before working. The following is a game for use at the start of class or rehearsal:

> Instructions: Members stand in a circle. Each thinks of a word. Going clockwise, each member says his or her word. Then, the director chooses members at random to recall the word of other specified ensemble members. The game is repeated with sentences. A flowing tempo is maintained.

The above game has multiple purposes: 1) it stops all activity that is irrelevant to the rehearsal/class; 2) it moves students out from behind their desks, gets them out of passive sitting positions, and brings them face-to-face with their classmates; 3) members learn each other's names; 4) everyone begins to listen in a very specific way, and to concentrate on the group; 5) the group begins to function as a unit; 6) good pronunciation becomes important; 7) as the game gets difficult, it becomes established that no one in the room is perfect, and that is a comfort to all.

Another game (called "Cup Ball" by the actors at the Station Theater in Urbana, Illinois where I often played it), is an enjoyable ensemble warm-up. To play, a paper or Styrofoam drinking cup is thrown into the air in the middle of a circle of actors. The actors try to see how many times they can hit

Cup Ball

the cup back up into the air before it hits the ground. No person can hit the cup more than once at a time, i.e., two hits in a row by the same person ends the counting. The counting also ends when the cup hits the ground. Each rehearsal may start with this game. As the weeks pass, the group will achieve higher counts. Cup ball contributes to the development of effective communication within the group. A vocal ensemble is formed, as players count aloud in unison with each hit of the cup.

For language learners, the game can have extra meaning. Counting can be done in the second language, or the numbers can be replaced by any other words that are being learned. Each hit could be counted by the name of a month, for example, and the object could be to see how many years a group can get through before the cup hits the ground. Or, the people who actually hit the cup each time could be the only ones who speak, e.g., one hitter could call out a sentence subject, and the next hitter must finish the sentence supplying, of course, the appropriate verb form.

Role Playing

Role Playing is also a game in the sense that participants play within the confines of previously determined "rules" or scenarios. Role playing is not performed for audiences, but it is used in rehearsals to give actors the opportunity to explore alternative solutions to characterization problems without the pressure of entertaining an audience. Two goals of role playing are to expand the actors' vocabularies of behavior and to increase their comprehension of a wider range of behavior in others.

The actors in the days of the Commedia dell'Arte used role playing to develop their talents and to create their scripts through improvisation. The actors experimented with the language and the behavior of their characters by role playing. It was a means of trying new things, discovering strengths and weaknesses, separating the good from the bad, and developing the good in order to shape a performance. In the Commedia, the performances were often improvised, but the actors were secure in their roles because they were experienced role players. Each actor role-played his or her character using as a basis the exaggerated, stereotypical norms established for each particular type; e.g., lovers are jealous, merchants are stingy, noblemen are foolish and vain, fools have insight, and so forth. The actors used role playing to discover, practice, and perform language acts to meet their audiences' expectations. "Life" was put on stage to be satirized and ridiculed, but also to be examined, evaluated, and reevaluated. The stage was not only a conveyor of humor, but also a conveyor of politics and education.

Although the characters that the Commedians role played were stereotypes, the stereotypes had entertainment value precisely because the audience and the performers were familiar with the real-life characters upon which the comic characters were based. This should not be forgotten when role playing is used to learn about and illustrate real-life roles. The role playing may generate oversimplified, exaggerated, or stereotypical characters, and there is nothing wrong with that as long as the learners understand the real characters upon which they are based.

In the language classroom as in the acting rehearsal, role playing, accompanied by feedback from the director/teacher and other ensemble members helps students/actors to learn to distinguish between what they feel is, or should be, happening, and what really is happening. Through role playing, actors learn to know themselves and they try to develop an awareness of how others perceive them. Role playing activities can be designed or adapted to isolate and illustrate a variety of teaching points, whether it is to teach culture or to give students practice with empathic communication skills, new intonation patterns, conventional speech formulae, nonverbal behavior, etc.

In many language teaching situations it helps if role playing activities are clearly structured. Students do not need to be given scripts with their lines written out, but the tasks they are asked to do should be straightforward. Improvisation can be difficult if the players' tasks are not clearly defined. Language teachers should consider the difficulty of the role playing activity before asking students to improvise. This is particularly important when the ensemble is still forming. It is a good idea to begin a course with non-threatening activities and gradually move into more challenging, self-revealing activities as the learners begin to develop a sense of security in the group. If they know a role playing activity will help them, and if they have the language skills to play their roles, most learners will enjoy role playing.

Role playing can manifest itself in a wide variety of activities. It can take a simple form such as having students react to an instruction like "Suggest to your friend that he stay off the city buses after midnight," or "I need two volunteers to take the roles of two residents of the same city who are disagreeing over whether or not it is safe to ride on public transportation after midnight." Role playing can also take the form of more complex simulations involving a cast of ten or more. For example, students may play the roles of participants in a town meeting searching for solutions to complex issues involving conflicting interests. Role playing can be designed to suit a group's language learning needs.

Criticism

Within the safe ensemble atmosphere, the director promotes an impulsive style, and so should the language teacher. The impulsive language learner may make more frequent mistakes than the laboriously reflective speaker, but he or she probably communicates more overall. The teacher can lead the class to use errors and mistakes as learning devices, but, like the director, the teacher must read the students' reactions constantly and be ready to turn the course of events to a more positive note if a learner becomes too uncomfortable. Students should never be made to feel too embarrassed or to feel that they have failed in any sense. Some proponents of the now infamous audio-lingual method went overboard on this point by never allowing students to attempt to use structures that had not yet been presented in drills. They failed to recognize that the students' own creative formulations, or *inter-language* are an important aspect of second-language development. Learners must be encouraged to make the best use they can of their second-language resources so that they gain the confidence and experience necessary to develop an even greater level of competence.

Students need not be perfect, since they are probably not perfect in real life. The teacher can approximate life by letting students get into trouble using the second language, and then by letting them see that they can get out of trouble through their own devices. Students in role-play situations, for example, may talk themselves into corners, unable to find the structures they are searching for. They then discover that by persisting and asserting themselves, they can eventually make themselves understood. In the safe ensemble atmosphere, students develop confidence and learn to cope.

Directors often take pains not to correct too much in drama rehearsals, realizing that role acquisition is a process that takes time. Criticism and correction are important, however, and need to be well placed. Language learners, like actors, are influenced by the consequences of their actions, and "rehearsals" are where those consequences should be felt. For actors, rehearsals are working situations quite different from performance situations. In rehearsals, the pressure to perform must be put at a distance. The actor will experiment with a role, drawing criticism from the director. Actors take safe, tried-and-true paths in most performances, but in rehearsal almost anything is worth trying at least once. Language learners commonly suffer from the opposite syndrome. They are too careful and reflective in the classroom and avoid exposing their ignorance and attracting criticism. Then, outside the classroom, they often speak quite freely. They should be encouraged to experiment in the classroom, and they should expect, appreciate, and make use of the teacher's constructive "criticism."

Monitoring

People do not always indicate to foreigners when they are performing badly. Since audiences no longer throw tomatoes at actors when they are performing badly, actors must learn to monitor themselves, and they count on monitoring from the director and fellow actors.

In describing the differences between "language acquisition" and "language learning," Stephen Krashen (1977) emphasizes the fact that adults make use of their ability to monitor themselves as they speak a foreign language. Whereas young children seem to "acquire" language skills with little visible attention to correctness or errors, adults "learning" languages monitor their own output. Whether adult language learners monitor themselves in order to correct errors or in order to avoid making errors depends on the individual. Probably most learners are motivated by both the desire to correct and the desire to avoid. The adult tendency to monitor language output can be a disadvantage in that it promotes heightened inhibition and loss of childlike spontaneity. It can be an advantage in leading to an analytical understanding of the language learning process. Ideally the language learner should be able to use analytical skills to monitor output without losing spontaneity.

Actors work to develop relaxation monitoring skills. For example, actors take movement courses to learn about the body and what it can do and to practice controlling their bodies. Unnecessary tension inhibits spontaneity. Actors use exercises to help them relax. Alternating between tension and relaxation of different sets of muscle groups, one can learn to control tension. To relax onstage, actors go through a process of chasing, locating, and minimizing tension. The more experienced an actor is at doing this, the more automatic the process will be. The more the actor can free himself or herself of tension, the more freedom will be left for expression.

The following quote (McGaw 1980) refers to the development of monitoring skills by actors.

Through systematic work, an actor will develop a "controller" inside himself that will instantly find the spot of unnecessary tension and as instantly eliminate it. This process of spotting must be developed into an automatic habit in life as well as on the stage.

Monitoring can be encouraged in the language classroom in a number of ways. In role playing or dialogue reading, for example, when attention is focused on intonation, students can be made aware of just how important intonation can be. Students may think they are expressing a particular emotion or attitude, for example, while because of their intonation, they are actually expressing a different, unintended message. As an example, the following is a fictional exchange between a language learner and a teacher who is using a theatrical approach to instill self-monitoring in the learner. (Learner is midway through the reading of a dialogue.)

Teacher: Wait a minute! Excuse me, but why do you think your character just said to his girlfriend, "I saw you with Tom last night"?

Student: Because she had told him that she couldn't go out on a date with him because she was sick, and he wants her to know that she didn't get away with her lie.

Teacher: How does your character feel about her having lied to him?

Student: His feelings are hurt.

Teacher: Is he angry too?

Student: Yes, of course.

Teacher: OK. Good. I think you're right. Your character is hurt and angry. But when you said, "I saw you with Tom last night," it sounded like you were greeting your milkman or waving to your paper boy, but you didn't sound like a hurt and angry boyfriend confronting his unfaithful girlfriend. Try it again being conscious of intonation, and be careful of where you look and your facial expression.

Notice that the teacher did not tell the student how to achieve the desired results. There are many different executions of the line that would work. What the fictional teacher is attempting to do is help the student "see" what it is he looks like, and help the student realize that this type of dialogue work is more than a vocabulary reading exercise. It is an exercise in communication. This is not to say that teachers should not give students an overt explanation of stress and intonation patterns, they should. I am suggesting that after students have some understanding of intonation patterns of the second language, they can benefit from monitored practice in using them.

Giving the performer's classmates monitoring tasks actively involves them in the monitoring process too. Groups within the class can be assigned to observe and report on different aspects of a role play, dialogue reading, or other interaction activities, e.g., appropriateness of intonation, gestures, eye contact, pronunciation, word choice if the scene is improvised, structure, and so forth.

In her book, *Communicative Competence—An Experiment in Foreign Language Teaching*, Sandra Savignon (1972) describes French classes that were in some aspects very much like acting classes. She said, for example, that the optimum group size for role-playing situations is about ten. This always provides an audience, i.e., the class members not participating in the interaction; yet the audience is small enough to feel a part of the interaction, thinking all the while about what they might say if they had the floor at the time. Acting classes are set up the same way, and much of the experience one gains is through observation—active observation, analysis, decision making, and evaluation of others' performances. Much comes to the minds of the audience that a performer does not have time to think about.

DEVELOPING COMMUNICATION SKILLS: THE INDIVIDUAL

Method Acting

When you are going to use role playing, dialogue work, improvisation, scene study, or play production in a language class, you need to set up the situation. You cannot simply ask the students to stand up and "act"; you must give them tools. To help in this endeavor, we will look at *method acting*.

Method acting was developed by the late Constantin Stanislavski, director of the Moscow Art theater. His books on acting theory (1936, 1949) are still highly regarded. Method acting involves establishing the true emotions and motivations of a character, then producing those emotions truthfully, that is, really creating those emotions inside—feeling them as you are acting them.

The method actor, like the language learner, is not as concerned with the words that come out of the mouth as with what those words mean to the speaker, why those words were chosen, and what the words mean to all who hear them. The actor looks to the inner character for answers. To understand the inner character, the actor must learn the details of the charactor's life, his or her culture, background, philosophies, loves, hates, and fears. Only after learning all these things about Hamlet can an actor truly know what is meant when he says "To be or not to be."

A person learning about a foreign culture needs to become a better actor in much the same way. All good actors study the characters they play in depth. The foreign student in America, for example, should be motivated to study the American character. In drama rehearsal, students practice character study, and if the script is an American play, the students study American characters.

Observation

Observation must become a habit if one is to become adept at character study. Actors study the specifics of a character and should not be satisfied with generalities and stereotypes. An actor's superficial or "surface" manifestations of character should be the result of an understanding of the "deep" character. Using class time to delve into "deep character" not only facilitates the study of culture, and the use of the second language for discussion and analysis purposes, it also gives the student an awareness of how deep character is manifested in surface behavior; that is, it gives students tools for use in the world of cross-cultural interaction.

The key to observation exercises is that they are deceptively simple; their purpose is to study detail. For example, during a rehearsal for a play, an actress reported to the ensemble about one of her observation journeys. In the play, she played an elderly, retired, first-grade teacher who had never married. The actress wrote a description of her character based on what her character says and does in the play, on what is said about her by the other characters, and on the italicized stage directions that comment on the character, telling the actress how she should say her lines and so forth. The actress then arranged to meet some women who were similar to her character. The actress took notes as she talked with them. She noted not only what they said, but what they did with their bodies—their hands, their posture, how they walked—and their mental states, eye contact, sound of the voice, and so on. Then she tried to build those characteristics into her own characterization. Stanislavski discusses the process of building real characteristics into an imaginary character in *Building a Character* (1949) and *An Actor Prepares* (1936).

Empathy

Empathy is the basis of method acting. Actors must empathize with their characters. In addition, actors, like language learners, need to be aware of how others perceive their actions. They need to learn what it is they should do in order that those watching them accurately perceive the message they wish to communicate. They need to develop empathic communication skills.

Horwitz and Horwitz (1977) discuss the importance of empathic communication. The utility of empathic communication for language learners is made quite clear, and it is suggested that the teacher take an approach that will facilitate an appreciation and development of empathic communication skills, as opposed to trying to teach the student every language situation in which second-language speakers are likely to be misunderstood.

Empathy, Horwitz and Horwitz point out, is essential for true communication. Taking the other's perspective in a conversation might enable one to continue a conversation in a meaningful fashion.

There is a certain amount of ambiguity concerning what an individual should say in a given circumstance. Because we are not able to participate in the experiential world of the other person, the precise relationship between our own and the other person's definition of the communicative situation and its respective roles can never be known with absolute certainty. A gap is likely to exist between our own definition of the situation and the other person's, because each of us perceives the world somewhat differently. [1977]

Horwitz and Horwitz recommend strategies for increasing empathic communication skills: "clarification," "content reflection," and "feeling reflection."

They point out that empathic communication minimizes our tendency to respond to people as cultural stereotypes. In responding to a speaker, if we use responses that reflect or attempt to interpret what we think the speaker means, then we give the speaker a chance to correct our misinterpretations or reinforce our accurate perceptions of the message.

Actors working on a script are continually trying to empathize with their characters. This task can be one of the greater challenges an actor faces in developing a role, especially if the character is quite different from the actor. How, for example, is one to empathize with Oberon in Shakespeare's *A Midsummer Night's Dream* if one has never had the experience of being "king of the fairies" in a forest outside of medieval Athens? Yet, the actor who is playing Oberon must empathize. In addition, the actor must empathize with those around him, at least to the degree that Oberon empathizes. The actor must come to understand with whom Oberon empathizes, to what degree, and why.

These in-depth analyses of character probe deeper than one normally probes when considering individuals one encounters in daily life. Actors working on a script, though, must concentrate on this aspect of human behavior and discover the empathic make-up of the characters in the play. When the script does not yield the answers, then the onus is on the actor to create the missing facts that will be consistent with the other circumstances of the play. A complete person must emerge from the actor's study of the character.

Some people are naturally more sensitive to relative degrees of empathy exuding from people around them, and others are less so. Since, as Horwitz and Horwitz point out, an appreciation of empathy and a control of empathic communication strategies is so important for the foreign language student, it makes a great deal of common sense to put our students through the same processes an actor goes through—that of role analysis and performance. Why performance? Because, after the student has come to understand the advantages of using empathic communication strategies, it is helpful to practice them.

Perhaps there is not enough classroom time to role play empathic communication scenarios until they are mastered, but two approaches are justified. One is to role play a few empathic communication examples for the sake of establishing what exactly we mean by "empathy" (experiential approach), and the other is to focus on empathic communication in every role play, scene, or play a class works on. The concept of empathy should always be present during the work being done on other points of focus in drama rehearsal.

All characters should be developed keeping in mind their capacity for empathy toward each specific person with whom they are interacting. For example, in the following role-playing scenario, the sales clerk displays a low level of empathy toward the customer. The participants in this scene should be made to understand the lack of empathy the clerk exhibits and how this lack affects both the communication between the two, and the perceptions that the customer and sales clerk have of each other.

> Scenario: A customer runs up to the door of a gift shop at the moment that the sales clerk is locking up for the night. Breathlessly, the customer explains how he's been trying for two hours to find the store, but that he's been lost because he doesn't know his way around the city, and nobody seemed to be able to give him accurate directions, and the traffic has been terrible, and he's been trying to maneuver a stick-shift car around in heavy traffic for the first time in his life, and it keeps stalling, and he has to get back to the office before five with a gift for an employee who is going away and never coming back, and the whole office is depending on him. The sales clerk listens quietly, then says, "We'll be open at eight A.M.," and locks the door in the customer's face.

It is clear that even if the store clerk displays a higher level of empathy toward the customer, the customer still might not be allowed to come in and buy a gift after hours, but there certainly is room for the store clerk to be more polite. Perhaps by displaying more empathy he would seem more polite.

Now, let us suppose that the store clerk has just received a phone call that his father has just suffered a severe heart attack, and that the clerk is on his way to the hospital to be with his father. It may be that no matter how much he empathizes with the customer, there is a very good reason for him to close up shop immediately without allowing the customer to come in and shop. Since the customer has no way of knowing about the store clerk's father, he may simply come to the conclusion that the store clerk is unsympathetic and rude.

This example scenario and ensuing discussion of empathy points out the difference between *being* empathic and *displaying* empathy. The process of analyzing scenes (simulated interactions) in this manner brings the concept of empathy to the students' attention, and gives them practice in developing the ability to display it. A single scene can be replayed with different degrees of empathy each time, in order to explore possible relationships between characters.

The benefits of empathy can be further illustrated by discussion of the situation actors face when they must play a character that they despise. For example, to play the role of Hamlet's uncle, an actor must be able to empathize with the uncle even though he is a cold-blooded killer. Here, a distinction is clearly drawn between empathy and sympathy. One need not sympathize with him in order to empathize with him. A parallel emerges. The foreign student may be thrust into situations with natives who have certain behavior patterns with which the foreigner could never agree or sympathize. Knowing that he or she must interact with these natives, the foreigner may wish to try to develop an empathic understanding of their "strange ways." The knowledge that one can empathize without having to sympathize, that is, without having to compromise one's own values and beliefs, can ease the foreigner's own internal conflict, allowing him or her to use empathic strategies to keep channels of communication open. It is in potentially difficult cross-cultural situations when one needs empathic communication strategies the most.

Voice and Body Training

Once actors have decided what to do to communicate a message, they need to have the flexibility to do it. Actors, therefore, attempt to master their physical and vocal instruments.

Voice training and body movement are usually first in actors' training programs. Actors become familiar with their vocal and physical ranges, and they learn to control and expand them. In drama rehearsals or language classes, students have a need to develop an awareness of their physical and vocal abilities and habits. They can increase their range and flexibility in using these aspects of language as they are stretched by the demands of their roles.

Vocal Warm-ups

Actors warm up their voices before rehearsals and performances because they know that they will be asking more of their voices in the rehearsal than they ask in their daily lives. Hamlet uses his voice in a different way than we do. For the actor to be free to explore the possibilities for creation of Hamlet's voice, he wants to have his voice flexed and ready to move in all directions so that it will sound natural, and very importantly, so that the voice will not be strained and damaged. Speakers of foreign languages are making demands on their voices too. Different languages consist of different sounds. Learning to produce new vowel and consonant sounds and new stress and intonation patterns is not easy. Language learners can benefit from voice training.

Moving from one language to another is quite a feat for the human voice. Anyone who wishes to speak effectively in a new language should give his or her voice the respect and care that it needs. Our students' attention should be focused on their vocal apparatuses for the long-term benefits that result from the discovery that the voice is capable of more than people often think and for the short-term benefits of having the voice warmed up and operating smoothly during the course of regular classroom language practice. Exercises that develop the voice and explore its range and versatility are effective and simple. It is unreasonable to expect foreign students to be very flexible without them. Would anybody expect a runner to run several miles without stretching his muscles first? Vocal chords and resonating chambers of the mouth, nasal cavity, and head are composed of muscles and tissues, too. If we expect students to develop intonation patterns, vowel and consonant sounds, and dynamic levels that sound appropriate for the second language, then we must make their task easier by making them aware of just what it is that the vocal apparatus is capable of doing.

"Warming-up" is one use to which we can put pronunciation drills. If viewed from an anatomical perspective, choral drills can justifiably be used to "loosen" the voice and isolate given sounds for practice. But drilling in the classroom is just that: drilling. It is only a beginning and should not be confused with the teaching of pronunciation or grammar. Language teaching methodology that abuses drilling techniques by over-using them is worse than no drilling at all. Actors do, however, drill themselves, and they are drilled in groups by their directors. They use drills to step outside of their roles and practice particular elements of the total communication task. Drilling can be productive when used as an opportunity to explore one's vocal range. Pronunciation exercises help students develop control over the voice. For the actor, as well as the language learner, vocal flexibility is an important skill.

Theater-type vocal warm-ups and articulation and rhythm exercises can be used in language classes to demonstrate the range of the voice, to loosen it up making it ready for work, and to isolate and practice the difficult contortions we all discover in a second language. Learners can learn to take advantage of the different resonating areas of vocal production, to use new points of articulation, and to be aware of how breath control is the main element of voice control. Warm-ups also focus the group energy as the students begin to listen to one another in order to perform the warm-ups in unison.

Physical Warm-ups

Physical warm-ups, e.g., stretching, calisthenics, are also taken quite seriously by actors. Such warm-ups relax the actors mentally as well as physically. Although students in many language-learning situations would not view physical warm-ups as a "credible" language teaching technique, even the most skeptical participants can learn to see the point of physical warm-ups as a language learning aid in the drama rehearsal. Warming up can help language learners gain an awareness of and control over themselves, which can make them confident. Confidence building is an integral part of acting and language learning.

Although an actor's goal is to be the master over his or her physical and vocal instruments, different actors experience different degrees of success. We know that in the course of most language courses we cannot turn out native-like second-language speakers. We are concerned, rather, with helping students make progress in the direction of the competent second-language speaker. It is not necessary to measure success in terms of native-like fluency. Similarly, it is not necessary that all students achieve complete control over their physical and vocal apparatuses in order to be considered successful. We are concerned that students improve their ability to communicate by improving their ability to control their communicating instruments.

Ear Training

Language learners with an awareness of the human voice and its capabilities can put their powers of observation into play if they can spend time in the world of the native speaker. They must learn to listen to and analyze the vocal patterns that are characteristic of the native language. Second-language learners should be equipped with the sensitivity to hear the intonation patterns of native speakers and to learn, on their own, the varied and expressive intonation patterns that are appropriate in different situations.

Can language learners really be expected to learn so much from listening? Can they be expected to actually produce the sounds they hear? We can gain insight into the relationship between acting and language learning by looking at the relationship between language and music and music and acting. There is clearly an analogy to be made between music and structural linguistics. There are phonemes (notes), phrases, intonation patterns, and discourse in music. There is also anaphora, paraphrasing, and the listener's "pragmatic expectancy grammar" (Oller 1979). There is a grammar in music—a grammar that the musician can describe, but which also communicates to many who cannot describe it. It is also true that, sometimes, one can neither describe the grammar nor comprehend the meaning of certain music because one has not previously been exposed to such music.

Members of different cultures are exposed to different types of music. Thus the capacity for any person to hear the subtleties of pitch, rhythm, and musical line is a function not only of that person's previous exposure to music, but a function of that person's culture, that is, a function of the type of music to which that person has been exposed. Westerners, for example, often listen to oriental music with wonder at the mysterious sound. They are unaccustomed to hearing the type of music that is common in the Orient. Many westerners do not know how to listen or to interpret the foreign-sounding music. On the other hand, the western ear is often quite used to listening to a symphony by Mozart or Beethoven, and the listener is frequently moved emotionally by it. What it is that moves an audience when listening to familiar music is a question for musicologists to investigate. The parallel is clear enough for the linguist and the language teacher.

Musicians, concerned with learning the "grammar" of music, make a conscious effort to develop their "ear," that is, their capacity to distinguish small nuances of pitch, rhythm, and musical line. They call the exercises they do "ear training."

The better a second-language speaker is at exploiting this capacity for aural perception, the better he or she will be able to hear and imitate what native speakers are doing. The goal is to reach the point where he or she can meet the native listener's expectations and thereby be comprehended. In order to help language learners hear and interpret the tones, pitches, rhythms, and lines of a foreign language, the teacher must help them to develop listening discrimination capacity through ear training.

Whether or not people can be trained to discriminate sound and reproduce it is a matter open to debate. Some contend that a certain amount of talent is required and that those born without such talent will never become good mimics. Others claim that, although talent is certainly a factor, most people can at least improve their ability. This argument is based on the notion that most people do not use their full sound discrimination capacity, and most people have not developed their potential ability to manipulate their sound output.

Purcell and Suter (1981) construct a profile of the good and poor pronouncers of English. The good pronouncers are also good mimics according to their idealized profile, and the poor pronouncers are poor mimics. This relationship is not surprising. Purcell and Suter, however, overlook the established practices of actors and musicians the world over when they say

> . . . aptitude, for oral mimicry seems beyond the control of the instructor; it is doubtful that one can make a good mimic out of a naturally poor one. This seems to match the common view that some people simply have a better "ear" for pronouncing languages, and that there is not a great deal language teachers or learners can do about it.

To acknowledge that talent is a major factor in mimicry and sound discrimination is not to concede that everyone has, through experience, already developed his or her full potential for sound discrimination and mimicry. Aaron Copland (1952) expresses a view that language teachers should consider:

> Listening is a talent . . . and we possess it in varying degrees. Listening also implies an inborn talent of some degree, which again, like any other talent, can be trained and developed.

In addition to the benefits an actor receives from voice- and ear-training exercises, the overall process of the drama rehearsal puts the sounds of the play into the actor's tonal memory. The changes in intonation that a given line traverses throughout the rehearsal period are gradual, even when significant. Each time an actor retrieves a line for recitation, he or she is activating tonal memory. Actors use tone to help themselves remember lines, words, sentences, and feelings. They store discourse in their heads as musical lines. This constant use of tonal memory to store and retrieve lines of plays has the long-term benefit to language learners of helping develop an "ear" for pronunciation. The use of poetry, song, and rhythm exercises ("Jazz Chants" for example—see Graham in Recommended Reading and Classroom Materials) in the language classroom represents a healthy trend that makes productive use of the tonal memory.

Discourse

Actors must make the language of a play realistic. This is difficult to do since the language is not real but is written in a script; the same sentences are spoken in each performance. The actor's task is to overcome this artificiality. To do that, actors need to learn what it is that makes language real. Then they must practice making language real.

The fact that actors must closely examine the small elements of real discourse and the way in which they fit together highlights another strength of theater as a language-teaching device. Language learners also must attend closely to and practice the elements that combine to make real communication. Widdowson (1979) effectively argues for this type of approach to language teaching when he recommends the inclusion of poetry in the language classroom. He points out that poetry provides us with a way to develop students' awareness of discourse—how it is constructed and how it communicates.

The play script, like a poem, is only a portion of a whole. The discourse of communication is more than just the words in the script. The playwright does not provide all the background information and instructions for executing a play. The actors need to discover the missing elements. It is the actors, not the playwright, who create the final discourse by filling in the missing pieces. It is the actors, not the playwright, who eventually show the audience real, communicative discourse. Actors must "create and recreate discourse from the resources of linguistic knowledge" (Widdowson 1979). So must language students.

Widdowson's assertion (below) remains astute even if we replace the word *poetry* with the word *acting*.

> Once it is asserted that the ultimate aim of a language teaching course is to develop the ability to create and recreate discourse from the resources of linguistic knowledge, and once it is accepted that poetry can be represented as a kind of discourse in which these processes are particularly open to observation, then I think one can begin to see a way of reinstating poetry as an integrative element in language teaching.

Widdowson refers to the fact that students studying poetry are using and developing "interpretive procedures" to create and recreate discourse from the poem. Clearly, students must do this to create discourse from the script and to make a live recreation of discourse for their audience. The interpretive procedures that they must use and develop will become useful strategies for interpreting and communicating offstage as well. Students learn to perceive what is happening and understand why they perceive situations the way they do. In addition, students learn to ask themselves, "What can I do to assure that my 'audience' will perceive my message correctly?"

APPLICATIONS IN LANGUAGE TEACHING

The discussion up to this point has made it clear that language learners and actors, like language teachers and directors, have much in common. Knowing this, you, the language teacher, can seek to use theater methods and techniques in language teaching.

Language classes in which students work in groups on scenes from plays with the intent of performing the scenes for classmates or for the public, and groups of non-native speakers who meet to develop one-act or full-length plays, are obvious manifestations of theater methodology.

Through the experience of play production, teachers and learners find that they can enjoy the language learning process; they will realize that there is more than one way to learn a language and that the learning of languages need not be viewed as such a fixed and staid ritual. Students will volunteer their time and work intensely on language for hours a week. They will study, they will be creative in their search for solutions, they will willingly take on active roles in the class, and they will feel a personal success. Also, through this experience, the teacher will learn about the individual students as language learners and find ways to borrow elements from the drama rehearsal for use in more conventional language classes.

Understandably, it is not practical for many language teachers to direct plays since this is a very time-consuming way of working with language students. For teachers seeking other applications, there are ways to integrate aspects of the drama rehearsal into whatever type of language syllabus one is teaching. (Chapter 3 is devoted to materials for classroom use.) Of course, in the end, it is up to the individual teacher to find or create the applications that best fit his or her individual situation. All language teachers will be aided by an understanding of what exactly goes on in the drama rehearsal. The following chapter illustrates how language is taught in rehearsal and how the concepts that have already been discussed are applied.

Chapter 2

Language Teaching in the Drama Rehearsal: A Focus on Language Teaching Strategies

This chapter explains how language teaching takes place in the drama rehearsal. To provide examples, there are references to specific experiences I have had directing rehearsals for English-language learning groups. The purpose of these "International Student Drama Groups" is always two-fold: (1) to enjoy working in a group on a creative and artistic product, and (2) to improve the participants' English language skills.

THE DIRECTOR'S STRATEGIES

Providing Freedom and Direction

A good drama rehearsal combines two very important, but not necessarily compatible, elements of an ideal language-learning atmosphere. One element is that the learners are receptive to criticism and suggestion from the director. They respond to the director's guidance in order to correct errors and improve performance. The other element is that the group tends to remain relatively spontaneous and uninhibited in the effort to use new language and behavior and to develop communication skills.

When contrasting child language acquisition to adult language learning, we attach significance to the child's willingness to be socialized by adults. We can correct a child's nonstandard speech or coach a child as he is speaking, e.g., "not 'barking,' Johnny, 'mooing.' The cow is mooing"; or "Don't forget to say 'Thank you.'" In the adult world, on the other hand, it is less likely that an adult non-native speaker can be stopped, corrected, and then expected to continue without feeling self-conscious or annoyed. Like the successful language class, the rehearsal provides the atmosphere in which this type of unlikely interaction can take place. The director has a parent-like role with respect to the actors. The concept of the play belongs to the director, but he or she must communicate that concept to the audience through the actors. The director, therefore, has a hand in every moment of the rehearsal. When the way the language is being used is not in keeping with the director's concept, the director intervenes. This is not to say that the director dams up the flow of language from the actors, rather, in the cooperative ensemble, director and actors work together to maintain a creative output, which is steadily being shaped into the director's concept of the play.

Viola Spolin, author of the widely read text *Improvisation for the Theater* (1963), talks of the approval/disapproval type of structure in our education and indeed in our daily lives. Our constant striving for approval results in an authoritarian relationship between the teacher and the student. In the rehearsal it is important to be spontaneous so that the intuition is free to create. Therefore, there must be a kind of equality between actor and director, or between teacher and student. This type of equality exists in game playing, where everyone is equal, yet plays within the agreed-upon limits of the game.

Equality in the teacher-student relationship seems difficult to establish. Spolin points out, "The teacher must often sit out the discoveries of the student without interpreting or forcing conclusions on him." Spolin reminds us that the director/teacher is more experienced and that his or her knowledge is needed as a guide, but that although the teacher/director may have "100 ways to solve a particular problem," the first-time actor may very likely come up with a 101st way. If the director tells the actor everything, then the actor is merely solving the problem within the limits of the director's knowledge. The object of this way of working is to try as a group to go beyond the knowledge of each individual to a collective, creative experience.

Many directing experts recommend that the director not provide approval too freely. If the actor gets approval too soon, he or she may settle for less and will have solved the problem in the director's eyes only. Directors, at chosen moments, withhold approval for fear that it will stop a growth process in midstream by causing actors to relax too soon before all discoveries have been made. For actors to develop an intuitive sense that will allow them to be creative, they must learn to decide for themselves whether or not a solution has been reached. Spolin reminds us that the giving of approval can be a manifestation of authoritarianism, which is undesirable.

On the other hand, actors must be given direction so that they know when they are doing something right, so they feel that they are learning something, and so they continue to know what is and is not in harmony with the director's concept of the play.

For many directors this is a cross-cultural problem in the sense that the director is in a "foreign" culture in the drama rehearsal—even if all the actors are members of the same culture as the director. It is the approach that is foreign. That is, it may seem to be a contradiction to be the group leader, instructor, and authority who must get the actors to realize a single artistic interpretation while at the same time allowing the actors the freedom to develop their own ideas, even if this means withholding instruction, approval and disapproval at times. Realizing that many cultures are permeated with an approval/disapproval definition of success is the first step in understanding the new rehearsal environment. Becoming aware of how this type of teacher-as-omnipotent-ruler structure could retard the creative process is the second step. The third step is realizing how the creative process facilitates an ideal language-learning atmosphere. The final and most difficult step is to implement the type of atmosphere in which the actors are free to operate according to their personal learning styles, while the director retains firm control of the group. Language teachers who are learning to direct will have to admit that they themselves are learning new skills and that therefore they must be patient and willing to take the time to recognize and break inappropriate habits.

The Stop-and-Go Rehearsal

In the stop-and-go rehearsal, as actors interact in realistic situations, the director can intervene to correct or instruct without stifling the actors' creative output. In preparing a play for performance, approximately two-thirds of the rehearsals involve stop-and-go work. Typically, as the players are rehearsing the play, the director stops them when there is a problem that needs to be worked on, or when he or she has something to add. Without breaking concentration, the actors listen to what the director has to say and perhaps a short exchange takes place between actors and director. When the point has been made, the director indicates where in the script the actors should resume acting. This is usually at some point that will lead them back into the problem section so that the actors can try the director's suggestion, and the director can see the result.

During these rehearsals the director may also "side coach," i.e., stand near the actors and talk to them as they are acting. Again it is important that the actors maintain concentration. When receiving side coaching, the actors should not "break stride."

Directors sometimes change the pace of rehearsal in order to achieve a desired result. If, for example, the actors are quite difficult to understand, the director might decide that their voices are not properly warmed up. He or she may then stop work on the play itself and put the cast through a series of vocal warm-ups until the cast is articulating more clearly and with ease.

If a rehearsal is progressing at a very slow pace and the actors seem uninspired and cannot keep up a moderate pace, the director might stop the proceedings and put the actors through a game, or a "line speed-through," in which the actors sit and read the play aloud as rapidly as possible until their energy level is higher. Then when they resume work on the script, they should have no trouble moving along at a lively pace. (*Note*: Line speed-throughs should be used only after the actors know the play reasonably well and at least well enough that they have no doubts as to the interpretation of the lines. Another purpose is to quickly refresh the actors' memories regarding the sequence of events in the play and the actual wording of the lines.)

The Notes Session

Another technique directors use to help solve the language problems of a cast is to take notes throughout the rehearsal. If a problem does not warrant stopping the show, a director will often write a note to be delivered verbally to the actors at some later point in the rehearsal. The actors write down the notes and then work on the problems before the next rehearsal of the section

Notes Session, *The Patient*: The director gives actors notes taken while watching the rehearsal.

in question. Once they are brought to the attention of the actors, many problems will disappear without the need for further explanation from the director. The more skilled and experienced the actors are, the less explanation is needed.

The director must find an optimum balance between giving too many notes for the actors to assimilate at one time and giving too few notes, thereby allowing the actors to continue making the same errors. In addition, some directions should be given immediately, and some should be saved for later. Each group of actors has its own tolerance level for stop-and-go rehearsals. Some actors can maintain a productive level of concentration in stop-and-go rehearsals longer than others. The closer a show is to performance, the more motivated an ensemble is to maintain concentration while the director intervenes.

Creative Thinking

Edward Debono (1967) describes a "lateral thinking" process that is the antithesis of "vertical thinking," i.e., logical thinking in which solutions are reached by a step-by-step procedure. The theater process counts on such lateral, or creative, thinking. Developing a character is often less a matter of thinking (in the logical sense) and more a matter of *doing*. From doing, the actor gains experience with a new character. Images begin to form in the actor's mind. Early in the process of character development, actors are not necessarily searching for what is right and wrong; they are just searching. They should be encouraged to let their minds roam. They should not try to find the straight-and-narrow path to a solution. Logic must be balanced with imagination.

The director's job is to free the actor to think creatively. The director should encourage the actor to experiment with a variety of approaches to a character. The actor will arrive at a thorough understanding of the play only after many hours of rehearsal. It is important that the actor become intimate with his or her character as soon as possible, taking liberties without waiting for permission and without analyzing at every turn what is "best." At the beginning of rehearsals, appropriateness is not as important as spontaneity. Images must be conceived, incubated, and grown. Later in the rehearsal process, the director will have to harness what has been created.

An important concept to bear in mind is that language, as we experience it in life, is not "linear." Neither is a play as the audience experiences it. After listening to someone talk or after seeing a play, we remember the message, but not necessarily the order in which the words were delivered. Rather than remembering the sequence of the words, sentences, and paragraphs from start to finish, we are likely to remember a collage of images that the language helped us to form. A linear presentation is not always the most simple or logical, or the easiest to understand. In fact, a strictly linear presentation does not take into account what our actual experiences with language are. Language should be represented to students with this in mind. Too much attention to form can make it difficult for us to remember what a given scene was about, just as attention solely to sentence-level structure deprives learners of the opportunity to learn about how and when a given language element is used and about what images it awakens in the native speaker's mind.

Actors and their director do not approach their play in a strictly linear fashion. The director's job is to take advantage of the actors' creative thinking potential and the non-linear nature of language. It is considered harmful to work on a script strictly from start to finish, if that means beginning with a total intellectual understanding of the play then finally working on the acting or realization of the language. Too much intellectual "talk" can lock the actors into bad acting patterns from which they may have great difficulty freeing themselves. The solution is to get the actors on their feet as soon as possible, before the play is completely understood. Indeed, it is believed that the play can be completely understood only when approached from this experiential point of view. The actors must not be allowed to study their script at length at home before the beginning of rehearsals. Memorizing lines too early will result in the actors being locked into intonation patterns and behavior patterns that are ill-conceived (based on an incomplete understanding of the characters and the action) and possibly inappropriate.

The director tries to help the actors discover, through images, the reality of the script. The script is not treated as written language, but as live, spoken human behavior. Early in rehearsals, the director might direct the actors to spend some time working on a few selected images for the play; for example, the actors might be directed to improvise scenes included in or suggested by the play, one from page 1, another from page 32, another from page 60, one from the closing scene, and so forth.

Sequencing

Teachers often ask themselves at what point in a language program it is best to introduce a particular element or lesson. In rehearsal it is best to teach specific language features when they are needed. This means that certain elements will be touched upon throughout the rehearsal period, and other elements will be taught only during specific sections of the rehearsal period. Vocabulary work, for example, is going to begin immediately as the actors are first learning the script, and it will probably continue being necessary until more than half of the rehearsals are completed. This may seem to be a long time for the cast to take to learn the meanings of all the words in the script, but since this is a truly integrated language experience, there are many different language concepts for the actors to think about at one time; the meanings of each individual vocabulary item will not necessarily be of primary importance at the start. Vocabulary, therefore, should be taught when there is a need for the actors to understand the items.

Articulation can be touched upon from the beginning. It should become especially important, though, after the cast is familiar with the basic story line and the characters. Work on articulation must begin early, so that by the time the performances start, the cast is well into the habits which make for clear articulation. This may involve changing speech habits that have been years in the forming.

Tempo and rhythm, of course, will not be in central focus until sometime later in the rehearsal period. These are elements that the actors will not be able to control until they are feeling secure in their characterizations, in the ensemble, and with the general flow of the show. The general flow of the show will not really be evident until individual sections of the script have received a substantial amount of individual attention. When the cast stops stumbling over their lines, tempo and rhythm become central concerns of the cast and director until the last minute of the last performance.

In performances, energy levels will be intensified due to the actors' awareness that they are being watched, and due to the feedback the audience gives the actors. The energy levels of performance will affect articulation, intonation, grammar, tempo, rhythm, and other language elements significantly. New sensations for the cast and director should be regarded as new information to be applied in the most beneficial manner possible.

Generally speaking, language teaching goes on throughout the rehearsal and performance periods. This is a highly integrated approach to language teaching, and therefore, most of the time, many elements of language are in focus at once.

LANGUAGE PRACTICE

Some of the most important language elements that are taught in the drama rehearsal were listed in Chapter 1. The following is a discussion of how each is taught. The language elements are described separately to highlight how specific language points are touched on in rehearsal. In reality, however, these examples are not so isolated; they are part of an integrated whole.

Grammar

The rehearsal reveals a wide variety of grammar errors that the teacher can work on by making them the focus of exercises, or by simply pointing out the errors, either at the moment they occur or in note sessions. Perhaps more is learned from a student's errors in rehearsal than in free conversation because in the play situation the director has a script. The script reveals what the student-actor means to say. The teacher-director then has insight into the "approximative system" (Nemser, 1971) of the student, who has revealed how he or she thinks a particular line should be said. Actors frequently speak lines differently than they are written in the script, even though they are holding the script in their hands. Once they are familiar with the script, they stop "reading" it on stage and use it only as a reference. Their approximative system often takes over as the actors speak thoughts instead of words. It will quickly become evident to the director that certain errors are occurring frequently. To illustrate, I have included some examples that actually occurred in my rehearsals.

In the sketch called "A Unicorn in the Garden" (Thurber 1962) the script reads

"I'm sorry sir. Your wife is as crazy as a jay bird."

An actor, who said the line correctly when closely watching the script, began to leave out the verb *is* when he had become familiar with the story, that is, he would say

*"I'm sorry sir, your wife as crazy as a jay bird."

In a different scene, from *The Long Christmas Dinner*, the actor who made the above error also made the following "errors" within a five-minute period:

Script reads:	"The snow is coming down like cotton."
Actor often said:	*"The snow coming down like cotton."
Script reads:	"You behaved like a spoiled brat, an ill-bred, spoiled brat."
Actor said:	*"You behaved like spoiled brat, ill-bred spoiled brat."

Since any given section of text is repeated often in rehearsals, it should soon become obvious to a director which problems are recurring. The above omissions clearly indicated that the learner was not completely in control of the verb *to be*, and that *articles* were a problem too.

How to rectify errors is a matter of individual choice. Simply telling the actor to remember the word might be enough to correct the errors in the play.

I am not suggesting that this will also solve the actor's habit of omitting articles in free speech, but it is one way to monitor the actor's output. Since the director knows what is coming, he or she can wait for a particular section to be played again and note whether or not the actor has corrected a given problem.

The repetition by the actor of the same text is not the same as the type of repetition required of students responding in "pattern practice" drills. Each time actors "perform" a given section of a script, they do their best to actually speak, feel, and think their lines as if they were real conversation. The rehearsal process demands this of actors. In acting, although the scripts are

---

*Indicates incorrect construction.

contrived, the "communication" is created on the spot by the actors, and it is, therefore, "real" communication.

Since actors take notes at the end of rehearsal, the teacher has a forum for correcting any shortcomings that may need correcting. It may be desirable to include an actual grammar lesson in the rehearsal process. This is, of course, up to the individual teacher.

Lexical Vocabulary

Working on a play expands one's vocabulary whether one is a native speaker of the language or a foreign speaker. Since actors strive to perform the language as "spoken" language, they learn it as such. As explained in Chapter 1, actors must be students of language. The actor must learn to understand the vocabulary and its use in each play.

That the language students/actors are really "learning" the new vocabulary in rehearsal will be evident to the director because, at first, much of the vocabulary will have to be explained. Even after the words have been explained, it will take time before all of the new vocabulary items are used in such a way that the director can be reasonably sure the actors understand them. By performance time, the actors will understand all the vocabulary items that at first were stumbling blocks. At this later stage, the actors will also begin manipulating the new vocabulary in fine and subtle ways. It will become clear to the language-teaching director just how effective the theater process can be in vocabulary building.

The actors will also generalize and use their new vocabulary outside of the play context. Offstage, for example, actors use many phrases and words they learn from the play. For the most part, they use their new vocabulary correctly in these other contexts. The ensemble itself provides a reinforcing atmosphere for using newly acquired vocabulary. Native and non-native speakers develop an attachment to the language of a play they are working on. Typically a cast will develop into a "speech community," and the actors will feel a sense of camaraderie as they use the new language. This often manifests itself when lines from the show continue to emerge in the actors' speech offstage. Actors sometimes do this consciously and for effect, but always correctly, i.e., appropriately within the context of the conversation. This indicates quite a significant progression from the early days of rehearsal when the actors do not know what these "new" idioms and vocabulary items mean.

Another parallel is suggested here between language and theater. At the 1981 International Teachers of English to Speakers of Other Languages Conference, Stephen Krashen spoke of a "din" that second-language learners hear, or sense, inside their heads. This occurs as they get over their initial hesitancy to use a language and begin to feel a desire to use it. He described his own experience in which he was asked to speak German. After an initial "shyness," he began to speak quite freely. After some time, he continued to hear German phrases and words inside his head, even after leaving Germany. A similar "din" is sensed by actors during the time they are performing a play. The language and images of the play are like a noise inside their heads even when they are not in the theater. This suggests that learning to use a language and learning to perform a play share some sort of "psychological reality" for the learners. Two weeks after her first experience performing with a drama group for language learners, an actress/language learner remarked, "I'll never forget my lines, I know them so well." Furthermore several other actors in her group commented that lines from the play continued to surface in other contexts away from the theater. They had not only "learned" the language of the play script, but had learned language that occurs in real life.

Emotional Vocabulary

The concept of emotional vocabulary expansion is similar to that of lexical vocabulary expansion in drama rehearsal: the work actors do with emotions helps them to learn to understand and empathize with a wider range of emotions in other people. Actors learn about their own emotional vocabularies as they try to develop an "emotional set"—a range and variety of emotions belonging to a specific individual—that coincides with the emotional set of the character to be portrayed. Frequently, an actor must react emotionally to experiences that he or she has never had or cannot relate to easily. The actor must employ strategies to understand these strange emotions. The concepts acting theorist, Uta Hagen (1973), terms *"sense memory," "emotional recall,"* and *"substitution"* are tools that actors draw upon to accomplish these emotional tasks.

Sense memory is the process of trying to recreate a sensation which one has experienced sometime in the past. For example, if one is pantomiming the eating of an ice cream cone, one might try to feel as if the ice cream is cold when it touches the mouth, and that it is sticky when it drips down the hand, and imagine how this dripping might motivate one to eat the cone faster, and so forth. This type of thinking helps the actor create a physical manifestation that conveys to the audience that he or she is really eating an ice cream cone. The audience may not be aware of all the images that the actor has in mind, but if effective, the audience will receive a very convincing global impression of a person eating an ice cream cone.

Emotional recall is the process of recalling feelings that one has had in the past and "plugging them in" to the emotional set of the character to be portrayed. For example, an actor portraying a nervous suitor on his first date might find it useful to recall as accurately as possible how he felt on some of his first dates, especially if those situations really made him nervous.

If the first dating situation never made the actor nervous, then that actor might use substitution to create the emotion. *Substitution* is the process of taking events from your past and plugging them into experiences you have never had in order to better understand those experiences. For example, the actor who is eternally confident in his romantic life might substitute some other experience that made him nervous. A job interview that made him nervous might be substituted for the nervousness in the dating scene at first. Instead of recalling how he feels on a date, this romantically confident actor recalls how he feels when nervous. Eventually the nervousness will come from within the scene itself as the actor assimilates the character's true emotions, and substitution will no longer be necessary. Substitution is a device for making staged emotions real and helping the actor learn to empathize with the character.

Physical Vocabulary

Physical vocabulary, i.e., the actor's repertoire of gestures, is also expanded in the rehearsal process. Different styles of theater demand different physical vocabularies, as do different characters within the same style. The actor is unlikely to be in the habit of using all of the physical gestures appropriate for the character to be portrayed. Therefore, actors try to develop their physical versatility. The physical manifestation of a character will take time to develop. The techniques used to develop these characteristics will help actors expand their physical vocabulary and increase their understanding of a wider range of physical behavior in others. The search for physical ways to express the messages of the play will yield isolated gestures at first, but later as the character becomes more "real" and the actors make the vocabulary their own, it will become clear that they have learned new vocabulary.

In this discussion of vocabulary, it should be stressed that we are not necessarily interested in teaching the specific vocabulary of the particular play in order for actors to use that vocabulary in daily life. Indeed, in some cases that would look awkward. What is more useful to actors is that they are becoming better vocabulary learners and interpreters. They become more aware of what it means to have a "range" of vocabulary that is limited only by past experience, which is expandable, and which varies from person to person.

Culture

The teaching of culture is divided into two categories: *coping strategies* (Savignon, 1983) and *knowledge*. Knowledge about a specific culture is learned from the script and the circumstances of the play itself. Skills that are useful in cross-cultural interactions are developed in the rehearsal process.

The Teaching of Coping Strategies

Of the two categories into which we divide culture, i.e., *knowledge* and *coping strategies*, coping strategies are perhaps the more important, since it is not possible to teach students everything they will need to know about the target culture. The best thing we can do for language learners is to help them learn about culture on their own. Savignon (1983) discusses coping strategies as tools of "strategic competence," an important component of communicative competence. Strategic competence compensates for lack of linguistic, socio-linguistic, and discourse competence.

Perhaps the most difficult task a person faces when living in a foreign culture is the interpretation of experiences. The conflict that people experience when their native culture clashes with a foreign culture can obscure objectivity and sensitivity to the point where rational analysis of events is impossible. In Chapter 1, some of the tools with which actors bridge the cultural gap between themselves and their characters were discussed: the development of observation skills, an understanding of how deep character is manifested in surface behavior, searching for the underlying meanings of what people say and do, empathic communication strategies, and learning to construct behavior patterns for individuals and subcultures so that it is evident when people are behaving consistently or when some deviation is occurring. Practice utilizing these tools in the drama rehearsal benefits foreign students in their cross-cultural lives offstage too.

The work actors do on character development is a continuous process of searching for cultural cues and applications of knowledge. The cast invests time in the discussion of the cultural elements of the play. For example, actors are obliged to discover why their characters are choosing the words they are using. Appropriate forms are supplied in a script, but an actor, if doing the job correctly, must seek to understand why the forms are appropriate. Students in acting situations learn to view language in this way. A major part of language learning is learning to use appropriate forms. As there is often a choice of forms, it can be difficult for the language learner to choose the most appropriate, and it is, therefore, good for the learner to try to find out *why* certain choices are better than others.

Of course, a multi-cultural drama group experience itself is a cross-cultural learning situation simply because actors from different cultures work closely together. Many second-language classes consist of multicultural groups. When such a group is molded into a harmonious performing ensemble, strategies for cross-cultural adaptation are employed. The practicing of such strategies fulfills a need for those language learners who might spend several years or more living and working in multicultural situations.

The process by which I rehearse a group is naturally a very American one, and partly for this reason, it has not always been easy to gain instant cooperation from all members of the group. In one case, for instance, some of the university students who were working with me in a drama group had to learn to arrive at rehearsals on time. Punctuality, or lack thereof, is a well-known source of misunderstanding between Americans and non-Americans in a variety of situations. Americans' sense of time and its importance is frequently difficult to convey to people who, because of their own cultural background, do not view time in the same manner as Americans do. Since the drama rehearsal is a group-oriented activity requiring the coordination of individuals, "American time" is a very useful tool. In addition, since the students in this particular case were in the United States in order to pursue degrees in the competitive, tightly scheduled environment of the American university, there was value for them in coming to terms with this time-oriented difference. (This is not to say that the teacher has no obligation to learn about and adapt somewhat to the values, habits, and feelings of the students. Cross-cultural sensitivity is, of course, a two-way street.)

The group learned that the play would be a better product if we all agreed on some means of establishing when the group would begin working each day. The actors went through a period of conflict before learning this. Some actors were becoming irritated with others for not arriving on time. The others felt as if they were doing no wrong in coming late to rehearsals since, after all, this was an extracurricular activity. Later, it became evident that the group was functioning more in harmony as each actor became concerned that the group was not kept waiting and that valuable rehearsal time was not lost in waiting for actors to arrive.

The point to be made here is that it was not coercion by the director or fellow cast members that made the late-arriving cast members begin to conform. Rather it was the growing cooperation of the group, due to the growth of a common creation—the play—to which everybody began to feel an allegiance. The play gave the group an opportunity to discover a source of cross-cultural conflict and, over time, to work the conflict out of the situation. I do not believe anyone in the group actually changed his or her deep-seated concept of time and its importance, but the cast learned something about the value of finding a way and a reason to cooperate in spite of the existence of some very different feelings about "the way things are."

Since the day-to-day world of cross-cultural interaction frequently involves the type of conflict just described, we are justified in providing opportunities for our students to learn to deal with this type of situation. Working in a performing ensemble, learners are in a position to confront conflict in the group and deal with it. There is enough security in such a group that conflict does not always have to be hidden.

Cultural Knowledge

The more skilled the language learners/actors become, the more adept they will be at acquiring cultural knowledge. As an illustration of what I mean by "knowledge," the following is an incomplete list of questions dealing with the culture of the characters in the play *The Long Christmas Dinner* (Wilder). Answers to these and other questions should be examined to help a cast understand the characters in the play.

1. How and why does one "hold a person's chair" when sitting down for dinner?

2. How is more food offered and accepted or rejected at the dinner table?

3. How representative are the attitudes about wars in foreign lands that are reflected in the play, and how do these attitudes differ when comparing Americans' feelings about World War II and the Vietnam war?

4. How careful must we be not to make firm unchangeable generalizations about people's feelings in relation to topics such as #3 above?

5. How does the American independent businessman (say, the owner of a small but successful manufacturing company) feel about the federal government; for example, is he likely to be a Democrat or a Republican? Does he care who wins the presidential election? To what extent can such generalizations be made? Are there, indeed, norms in cultural behavior that can be described in this manner? What are the exceptions to the patterns we consider normal?

6. What happens to the nuclear family in the United States when children become adults? Why do many elderly people live away from their children? Has this always been the case?

7. How have some of the customs and ideals reflected in the play changed with the times? What will the native audience members perceive as "old fashioned"?

Preparing to perform a play can involve far more than rehearsing the script. For example, in order to acquire cultural knowledge for *The Long Christmas Dinner*, we prepared and ate a "Christmas Dinner" (in April!) complete with turkey, stuffing, mashed potatoes, cranberries, rolls, wine, coffee, and pumpkin pie. The actor who played the role of the father, Charles, was assigned the job of carving the turkey—something which he is supposed to do in the play, but which the actor had, in fact, never done. The dinner was also a technique for developing physical vocabulary. Since the actors did not eat real food during the play, that is, they had to pantomime the eating of a Christmas dinner, it was helpful for them to experience actually eating the food. This experience included seeing the food, passing it, feeling the relative weights and temperatures, speaking the language of dinner table interaction, and so forth. For some actors, it was a new experience to eat that specific combination of foods, prepared and served in such a fashion. For the characters in the play, as well as for many people in the United States, such a meal is a well-known ritual. At this "Christmas dinner" the conversation centered around the Christmas celebration. Those actors who were Moslem and Jewish and who do not celebrate Christmas at home probably learned the most about Christmas from the experience, but the foreign actors who do actually celebrate Christmas at home also learned some specifics about the American Christmas celebration.

On another occasion the cast helped decorate the Christmas tree that was a part of the set for the play. For two of the students this was their first experience decorating a tree. Such experiences contribute to the actors' overall image of the characters in the play and their culture. In the case mentioned above, the actors learned a great deal, not only about the culture of the play but also about the host culture in which they were actually living.

Language Functions

The rehearsal process is one of viewing the language of the play as a series of functions. The actors spend the early rehearsal periods determining what the various functions are in the play. The vocabulary may be clear, but the functions elusive. A language function depends on context and the individual situation. As the actors come to know all of the variables in a given scene, they are learning about the functions of the scene. The director guides the actors in this process, helping them to come to an understanding of the entire play and their characters through the language functions.

For example, in *The Long Christmas Dinner*, the son enters the room and the father says, "Roderick, I have something to say to you." The function of the line may not be obvious to the actors upon first reading the script. The function is to communicate to the son that he is about to be reprimanded, and that if he knows what is good for him, he will listen obediently to the father. When this function eventually becomes clear, the actor has learned about a significant aspect of the father's behavior, that is, he has learned about how the father communicates with his son when disciplining him. The other actors on stage must also understand this function so that they can react to it accordingly: The son must react defensively, and the other characters must react with embarrassment or irritation over the fact that the father is spoiling Christmas dinner. Upon first reading the script, actors might understand the meaning of the example sentence in isolation, but it takes a closer investigation to know that the father is not merely stating the obvious when he says, "Son, I have something to say to you."

After the actors understand a function, they must then learn how to perform the function in order to communicate the idea to the audience. This is no easy task. It is no wonder that when language students in conventional language classes read dialogues, they only perform superficial representations of reality. A realistic performance takes time to develop. An upcoming performance motivates students to spend time developing real acts of communication.

As they try to communicate the myriad functions in a play to an audience, actors learn just how subtle the process of communicating a given function can be. When they discover that functions other than the intended ones are coming across, they search for ways to alter the message they are putting out. They discover that many different aspects of communication can interfere with the intended message. They discover this primarily through feedback from the director, and later from the feedback of audience members, who may, for example, laugh at the wrong time. (Indeed the audience may laugh at the right time, leaving the actor to be the last to realize that he has been communicating a "joke" without knowing it.)

Subtext

All the work on the appropriate execution of language functions helps the actor learn to appreciate the subtext of the play and how meaning goes deeper than the surface meaning of sentences. The play is a complex web of meaning that the actor must first untangle, then present clearly to the audience. Attention must be devoted to reading between the lines of the play. The actor sees that the playwright's words are a mere framework for a larger, more complete event. The director and actors must fill in the blanks.

To this end, the director sometimes directs the actor to write down the "subtext" for a scene, e.g., the actor will write down what the character means as opposed to what he or she is saying, or the actor will write down what the character is thinking during a scene. In the process of trying to write these things down, the actor must make decisions about what exactly the character does mean at any given moment. Actors think in terms of "wants" and "desires." A director may ask actors to think about what their characters want in a scene.

Everything an actor knows about his or her character is not necessarily seen directly by an audience. All of the background elements of a character are, nevertheless, in some way affecting that character's behavior, just as all people are, in ways which are not always obvious to the casual observer, affected by their past experiences.

Intonation and Stress

Intonation and stress play a more significant role in speech for the stage than they do in off-stage conversation. Since intonation and stress are consciously manipulated by actors to communicate their interpretation of the script, when these elements are misplaced, the dialogue is often misunderstood or totally incomprehensible. The latter is likely to be true especially if the stress is not native-like and if it violates the expectancy of the native listener. Due to the exaggerated role of intonation and stress in stage speech, in contrast to off-stage speech, the actor has a stronger need than the non-actor to attend to these extralinguistic elements. This need is compatible with the need of the language learner who must pay attention to the stress and intonation patterns of the target language because he or she is learning the system. The language learner/actor is getting a special opportunity to become skilled at attending to stress and intonation problems because it is more important for the stage speaker than the off-stage speaker.

Misplaced sentence stress and intonation are perhaps the most serious obstacles standing in the way of the audience's understanding of the play. Actors have a real motivation to work on this problem because they realize that only if they minimize it will their hard work on all other aspects of the play pay off.

During rehearsals for the production of *The Long Christmas Dinner*, I observed one actor as he made significant progress in controlling his stress and intonation patterns. He was an Arabic speaker. At the beginning of the work on the play, he was often difficult to understand when he spoke English, even in one-to-one conversation. The two main obstacles to understanding him were his vowel sounds, which were short and clipped, and his lack of stress variation—all of his syllables were stressed the same. By the time the play was performed, this actor was comprehensible most of the time. He went through a progression starting from no variation in stress within sentences, to the use of a small amount of misplaced stress, to a large amount of misplaced stress, then to a significant amount of correctly placed stress and some misplaced stress. It is logical to assume that speakers of languages without the type of variation in sentence stress that English has will place stress in the wrong places when they first start placing it at all. I considered it progress when the actor mentioned above spoke the following sentence with the stress over the syllable *some*. It was progress, not because the stress was correct, but because there was any stress at all.

Example: "Roderick, I have *some*thing to say to you."

Although the above sentence sounded strange, the misplaced stress indicated that the actor was feeling less inhibited about experimenting with stress. Later, he was able to place the primary stress of the sentence on the word *say* as would a native speaker.

At one point in rehearsals, I noticed that an actress in the play was misplacing stress on several lines, all of which had adverbs of time and place at the end. This actress was also in the habit of putting primary sentence stress incorrectly on pronouns, giving her speech a foreign sound, which was often incomprehensible. Throughout the last few weeks of rehearsal, I pointed out to her in note-taking sessions that she should change her line delivery by stressing the adverb at the end, giving the sentences emphatic stress, and by stressing the word "two" for contrastive stress.

Example: "What? Have I got *two* invalids on my hands at *once*?"

I also pointed out that she was stressing pronouns, and that pronouns usually don't receive such strong stress. The actress made an effort to combat this problem, and gradually her misplaced stress disappeared from the sentences.

The following technique is useful for dealing with stress and intonation problems. During rehearsal, certain lines are repeatedly executed by the actors with non-native-like stress and/or intonation. Take note of the most distracting errors, especially those that make the actor's speech incomprehensible. At times, the director can work on a general problem by choosing two or three lines that are all manifestations of the problem. Instruct the actors in a note session to write out the sentences containing the problem. Then tell them to underline the syllables that should be stressed and to practice the sentences. Tell them the appropriate rule governing stress and intonation, if doing so will help. If the problem persists, insert the sentence containing the error into the group warm-ups at the beginning of rehearsal. Have the entire cast chant or sing the line(s), exaggerating the stress and intonation pattern. (See Chapter 3 for vocal warm-up ideas.) The whole group then becomes the monitor for the actor who speaks the line in the play. Usually this technique is effective in getting the actors to change their habits.

Below is an error made repeatedly by an actor in one of my groups as he spoke a line in his script.

ERROR: "You mustn't be depressed."
(Underlined syllable received major stress.)

To cure him of this, we used his line in our group vocal warm-ups at the beginning of several rehearsals.

NEW WARM-UP GIVEN TO WHOLE GROUP: "You mustn't be depressed."
(Underlined portion indicates major stress given to line by group.)

In addition to curing the actor of his distracting intonation problem, the warm-up containing this sentence served many of the other functions that warm-ups are supposed to serve, e.g., molding the group as a unit, tuning the actor's listening devices, loosening up the articulating mechanisms, and so forth.

Articulation

Through acting, language learners become better articulators. In rehearsal, the director constantly stresses clarity by emphasizing articulation, tempo, and volume. The actors learn that when they mumble, they are hard to understand. Most importantly, they have the opportunity to learn to control their articulation, which is not easy to do, since many of us mumble unconsciously in daily life. On the stage, one learns to be very conscious of articulation and to develop strategies to control it. The articulation necessary for clear stage speech is more exaggerated than needed ordinarily, but a good stage voice is natural in daily life. Foreign speakers of a language can benefit from having this type of control over their vocal instruments, since they so often find that they are misunderstood due to a variety of elements in their speech which may not meet the expectations of the native listener. Clear articulation can compensate for other non-native-like elements which make spoken language unclear. Skillful control of articulation is, thus, a useful tool for overcoming incomprehensibility.

Getting foreign speakers to attend very closely to articulation may be difficult in many other types of language classes, but in rehearsal it is something that the student actors clearly consider very important. As with all things in language teaching, students learn best when they feel that they have a need to learn. It is not unusual in rehearsals for a director to stop work on the play itself and put the group through a choral warm-up (drill!) in order to focus attention on articulation, and then resume work on the script.

Role Playing and Improvisation

It is suggested that if students are going to be asked to role play, they should first have a good reason for doing so. Actors have a good reason for doing so especially when it is in the context of drama rehearsal. Actors in rehearsal will do many things that people may not want to do in a regular classroom, because they sense that the activities will help them with the performance and understanding of the play. The more a person role plays and improvises, the easier it becomes and the more one can get out of it.

Role playing is used in rehearsal to give actors experiences and feelings that the script does not provide, but which help in the overall development of the performance. The experiences acquired during role playing often help the performance in a manner so indirect that the audience never knows how the effect is achieved.

For example, there is a scene in *The Long Christmas Dinner* in which the father reprimands his son for getting drunk and being rude in public at a Christmas Eve dance. The sister is the only member of the family who witnessed the "offense," and she defends her brother in the scene. A possible role play situation would find the sister and brother at the dance as the brother is carrying out the act that offends the father. The actors can decide for themselves how they feel about the father's accusation, i.e., Was the son really being rude?, How drunk was he?, etc. In the role play, the son can experience the "act" of being socially improper, and then, while working on the play, the son can have a real act in his past to relate to as he is defending himself against his father's reprimand.

At another point in the play, a child dies just after birth. One possible role play for early in the rehearsal period would be for the father and mother of that child to enact the conversation they might have had later that week as they talk about the lost child. In doing so, the two actors would explore the possible emotions of their characters with respect to this incident, and they would also add a dimension to their relationship as husband and wife. This experience in their past and the ensuing discussion will add substance to other scenes in the play.

It is important for the director to realize that these role playing situations are not performances. The actors need to communicate with each other, but it is not necessary for them to "project" the message of their role playing to anyone else. The object is to provide the actors with experiences upon which they can draw, that is, to give them experience being in their characters' shoes.

Role playing can be used to isolate many different elements of acting. The above examples isolate emotions and aspects of human interaction. Role playing could also be used to isolate non-verbal behavior, types of structures, or words.

Non-verbal Communication

As mentioned earlier, actors take courses in stage movement, modern dance, ballet, tai chi, and other types of movement training. Ideally, professional actors approach movement training as an athletic endeavor. They may devote many hours to working out and staying in shape. Instead of taking the time for extensive movement training when working with language learners in theater groups, one can focus on the *appropriateness* of the actors' physical actions as a means of developing the non-verbal aspect of the play.

Most of the non-verbal acting must be created by the actors themselves. The director can aid in the development of non-verbal acting by making suggestions and keeping the actors informed of how they look.

Some simple training exercises can give the actors an awareness that acting is a non-verbal task as well as a verbal one. One useful exercise which may be used in the early rehearsals is the "economy in acting" exercise. One at a time, the actors are instructed to "Walk to the chair, see the hat (or any object), pick it up, look at it, put it back down, and walk back to where you started." Each actor is told to repeat the exercise, and to "try to improve" each subsequent attempt. This exercise is designed to be difficult. Most actors cannot successfully complete it at first. They do not know that what the director is watching for is extraneous behavior that could possibly constitute communication of something besides the instructions. If, for example, the actor smiles upon looking at the hat, or if the actor looks out at the audience (fellow cast members assembled in a line of chairs) during the execution of the instructions, or if the actor looks around in a way that could communicate "I'm looking around," he or she will be asked to try the exercise again. Later, the point of the exercise is explained to the actors. The point is to demonstrate to them that everything they do communicates something, and that when they have a specific message to communicate, they must be very careful that they don't communicate something else.

After the point is made with the above exercise, the actors are ready to be coached in their non-verbal acting. Actors must choose their actions carefully, then execute them carefully, that is, make each action separate and complete, giving each one a beginning, a middle, and an end. The audience, then, will receive an unambiguous message.

Occasionally the director can suggest specific gestures for the actors to use, but, for the most part, actors should be left to find specific gestures on their own, since they are the only ones who can really create what is natural for their own bodies. The director's job is to "edit," by pointing out when gestures being used are working, and when they are not. The director must be conscious of what the actors are trying to do. An assessment must be made of each actor while rehearsing. When it is apparent that an actor has found a useful set of actions to go with a particular scene, the director should tell the actor that those actions are working well. If a director sees an actor struggling to find something physical, then the director should help out by making suggestions as to what type of gesture might be appropriate.

Acting is an integrated form of expression. It might be effective to help the actor find physical actions by discussing how the character feels at a given moment. Sometimes actors do not know what to do with their bodies in a scene because they do not know what to do with their minds, that is, they have not figured out how their characters feel about what is happening.

One exercise that helps to bring the nonverbal elements of the play to a higher level of awareness is what McGaw (1980) calls a "physical inventory." A physical inventory is similar to a film script, which lists each of the "takes" the camera must shoot. First, the actors run one scene in the play. Then they are told to write down everything they do during the scene. The script does not provide the answers to such questions. The answers come from the characters themselves. What kind of people are they? How would they feel if this were really happening? How would those feelings manifest themselves in surface behavior?

For example, the following scene appears in the middle of the play *The Long Christmas Dinner*.

Synopsis of Scene: The family, mother, father, daughter, and aunt (father's sister) is seated at the dinner table. The youngest son (18 years old) comes in for dinner, and immediately the father begins to reprimand the son for his rude public behavior at the Christmas Eve dance the night before. The son's initial reaction is to ignore his father by talking about something else. Then the son defiantly challenges the father to explain to him what it is he did that was "wrong." The argument escalates to the point where the father tells the son that he is withdrawing financial support for his college study, and expects him to come to work at the family factory after Christmas vacation. The son storms out of the room (never to return) and the scene ends.

Below are the transcripts of the physical inventories made by one group of language-learning "actors." After the actors write these, they perform the scene again. The director chooses a few physical inventories to read while monitoring the actors to see if they follow their inventories exactly. Typically their actions will follow their written inventories closely, but not exactly. The director and actors then discuss the additional actions they used and determine what it was that those actions communicated. The need to find new actions, and to eliminate unnecessary actions, is also discussed. This exercise is not done for every section of the play, but it is helpful to do it once or twice to make the actors aware of how precise they should, and can, be.

Examples of Physical Inventories:

Lucia: I look at Roderick while entering. Pick up the bread basket while listening. When Roderick refers to me, I look at him and respond with an air of not being interested in discussing the matter with him. I pick up the mashed potatoes. I serve myself a little, but I don't eat it because of the growing argument (between Roderick and father). I then look at Roderick, Charles, and Genevieve. Then, I look down while playing with my napkin since I feel embarrassed (over the argument). I wish I wasn't present. I realize Leonora is hurt, emotionally, so I go to comfort her.

Genevieve

1. I answer Lucia's question.
2. look at Roderick when he enters.
3. serve myself some dinner (without emotion).
4. listen to the start of the discussion.
5. slowly stop eating.
6. when Charles is really mad, I completely stop eating.
7. then I yell at Charles for ruining Christmas dinner.
8. then I just look at what everybody is doing.

Leonora: At the window, upset, thinking about Sam who just left (to go) to war. Roderick, my son, comes in apparently happy. Leonora worries because there will be an argument between father and son. The argument starts, I look upset and sad, and I'm terribly upset and desperate, trying to stop Charles. The argument develops while there is a heavy atmosphere at the table. Everybody is looking at each other, worrying, wishing that what's happening weren't happening. The argument is over. Roderick leaves, and I become desperate and sad for him. Lucia tries to comfort me, but it's too late to accept the truth.

Through exercises like the above, the actors monitor their non-verbal output carefully, searching for ways to communicate their messages and eliminating actions that distort their messages. This may seem to be a very unnatural way to behave; certainly in life we don't have the time to monitor our behavior so closely and edit our actions. What the process does for the actors is to bring non-verbal behavior to a higher level of awareness. It allows the actors to experiment with non-verbal acting as a medium of communication, learning, as they work, how to expand and control their own output. They also learn through constant monitoring by the director that their own output may not be as clear to others as they once imagined. They learn that misinterpretations frequently occur, and they develop coping strategies, like empathic communication skills, which help them determine what people are perceiving of them.

In the last weeks of rehearsal the actors' non-verbal performance of the play begins to look natural. This takes time. In the process, the actors become very aware of their non-verbal habits and begin to learn about what they are communicating. One student actress, for example, often shifted around from foot to foot when she was offstage, standing and talking to people. The more people seemed to focus attention on her, the more she shifted around. She soon learned that, onstage, this action was inappropriate for her character. It made her character look nervous when her character was not supposed to be nervous. The actress also learned that this was a very difficult habit to break. Eventually she found a means to control the habit for the time she was onstage.

Again, it is not a perfect mastery of bodily actions that we are striving for. We can help our students if we can give them an awareness of nonverbal behavior: how it communicates, how it is misinterpreted, and how in and/or out of control it can be.

Dynamics

Plays and scenes can be divided into "beats." Each beat is a main event that must occur and be seen clearly by the audience. The events are called beats because they provide a rhythmic plan of action. Each beat has a beginning, a middle, and an end and is a focal point around which the energy levels of the play ebb and flow. The division of the play into beats reflects the interpretation of the director. Giving the actors a list of beats familiarizes them with the script and helps them understand their task. At any given point in the play, the entire cast should be in agreement as to what the beat is about. (See List of Beats for *The Long Christmas Dinner*, Chapter 4.)

The speed of the passing beats creates the rhythms of the play. Within the rhythms, there are tempos of individual lines, cue pick-ups, sections, and actions. Tempo and rhythm combined are referred to here as "pacing." Onstage, pacing is a most sensitive variable, which can determine the actor's success in manipulating the audience.

I tell my students to think of the effects different types of music have on them: jazz, rock, classical, etc. Performers should think of themselves as a musical ensemble whose tempos and rhythms can generate feelings in an audience.

Warm-ups sometimes included a line speed-through in order to let the cast feel the play running at a very fast pace. As mentioned previously, in a line speed-through, the actors sit down and read or speak their lines as fast as possible, leaving few or no pauses. This not only helps them feel secure about their lines (my groups do this every night before performing for the public), it also gives them a sense of pacing; that is, it gives them a sense of what the play feels like at a different speed.

During the rehearsals, the director is constantly telling the cast to slow down or, more frequently, to pick up the pace. It is important that the actors develop a sense of pacing so that in performance, when the director cannot participate, the ensemble can work together to control pacing. The ability to manipulate pacing is a useful skill for all language learners to develop. What some language learners lack in pronunciation they can compensate for in pacing.

Listening

In the drama rehearsal there are different types of communication that the students are working to develop. There is the message of the play, which must be communicated to the audience. The actor who knows what the audience should perceive faces the challenge of seeing to it that the audience does, in fact, perceive the message accurately.

Another type of communication skill that actors must develop is that of communicating with the people onstage. When native or non-native English speaking actors work on a script, the early rehearsals will be characterized by speech that sounds like the actors are reading their lines or mechanically reproducing memorized utterances. What is lacking in the initial rehearsals is the sound and appearance of people talking to each other. Actors may get so preoccupied with speaking their lines, remembering where to walk, and when to talk that they forget that they are supposed to be talking to someone. At the same time the actors might not really be listening to each other. It is not until later that actors react to what other actors are saying. This implies that, eventually, the actors will be reacting to the manner in which the other actors are speaking their lines. Since each actor is developing a role, the characters on stage are usually in gradual transition. Those actors who listen well to each other as they act together will be developing characters who evolve together. The play will grow as a single entity and not as a series of one-performer acts. A new intonation pattern may contain a new cue, i.e., if an actor delivers a new intonation pattern, the other actors on stage may be required to respond in a new way. They must be *listening* in order to react appropriately to what the other actors are doing. Bad acting is frequently characterized by bad listening. Audiences know when actors are not listening to each other.

Role playing and improvisation require good listeners to be successful. Some groups of actors can improvise scenes so well that the audience does not realize that the scenes are unrehearsed; the actors listen and respond to what the other actors say and do and to the audience feedback.

The type of close listening and responding that actors must do in order to make the play "believable" for the audience is real practice in empathic communication. Within the confines of their characters, actors respond in a way which says, "I heard you, I know what you mean."

Student actors are being encouraged to use empathic communication skills when they are reminded to do things that are not spelled out in the script. For example, in *The Long Christmas Dinner*, when Lucia (mother) makes a reference to her feelings about her recently deceased husband, her son, Charles, has no lines written into the script with which to respond. His next line is "White or dark, Genevieve? Just another sliver, mother?" (he is serving turkey at dinner). The actor playing Charles in our production had to be reminded that when his "mother" speaks of her sadness over the death in the family, especially at Christmas dinner, which is usually a happy occasion, the son's only appropriate reply would be to somehow console her, perhaps by agreeing with her, or to show concern for her sadness. To simply offer more food to people at the table without some nonverbal response in recognition of Lucia's feelings would indicate to the audience that Charles was ignoring Lucia, or perhaps it would appear that he was intentionally indicating some sort of disapproval over her topic of conversation by pretending to ignore it. Neither of the latter responses would have been consistent with Charles' character—at least as the actor in our production developed Charles' character. In this case, since there was no verbal response written in the script, the actor had to somehow respond nonverbally.

An important skill for actors to develop is to perform as if the events in the play are happening "now." Although a play is rehearsed and performed many times, the cast must, at the moment of performance, create and perform what is happening. They cannot hope that performances created on previous days or nights will simply repeat themselves. When actors put themselves on "automatic pilot" and cease listening to each other, the play suffers, and the audience knows.

Performing

All of the problems that stand in the way of effective performance of the director's concept of the play are language problems. The director must realize that, even in the final performance of the play, there will be imperfections. If, for example, there are stretches of dialogue that the audience finds incomprehensible, there is no reason to believe that the drama rehearsal has somehow not helped the actors improve comprehensibility. The actors whose speech is difficult to understand in performances will have manifested their problems in rehearsal as well. Certainly the director will have been working to solve the problems in rehearsal. Whether or not one is able to turn out a perfect product in the form of a completely comprehensible stage performance is irrelevant. No other teaching method is able to turn out a perfect product either. The important point to be made here is that the problems that the audience sees are exactly the problems which the director works on daily in rehearsal. Perhaps the actors will not be excellent speakers, but their performances are certainly going to be improved after such intensive vocal work. Such approaches to language teaching, which so clearly underscore the needs of the learner for both learner and teacher to see, are rare indeed.

Another important consideration is that performing is a very stressful situation. The language errors actors make in performance are not necessarily part of their internalized systems. Even native speakers place stress in very unnative-like places in their utterances when they are performing in a play. Even native speakers who are very articulate offstage will have trouble making themselves understood when performing a play. Their problems are, frequently, misplaced word and sentence stress, inappropriate intonation patterns, speaking too fast or too slowly, speaking too softly, inserting pauses in unnatural places, and maintaining an inconsistent and unnatural tempo. Mumbling, that is, bad articulation, is often a problem. Regional dialect, which makes Hamlet sound as if he has lived most of his life in Brooklyn, can stand in the way of an actor's effective performance. Even native English-speaking actors contend with these language problems in rehearsal. The very urgency of these problems motivates the actors and director to work toward a solution.

In addition, the good, clear vocal production of accomplished stage actors is an elevated form of speech. It is not necessary that our students learn to do this well. But in the process of doing their best, they will be developing the valuable skills needed to manipulate their communicative instruments.

Chapter 3

Theater Techniques
for the
Language Classroom

. . . the techniques of the theater are the techniques of communicating. The actuality of the communication is far more important than the method used. Methods alter to meet the needs of time and place.

—Viola Spolin

The uses of the theater arts in language teaching are potentially as varied as the collective imaginations of language teachers. This chapter offers exercises for use in the second-language classroom. In collecting them it has been considered that teachers most often do not have the luxury of many hours of preparation time at their disposal. Many programs cannot, practically, accommodate a class devoted entirely to theater techniques. The exercises in this chapter have been chosen because they fit into busy classroom programs. The following exercises illustrate applications of the ideas presented in the previous chapters. They are meant to serve as examples and to suggest ways for readers to create applications of their own for a variety of teaching contexts.

No single teacher is likely to use all of the exercises presented here. Some of them will not be appropriate for your situation. Your choice will depend on your class. In some cases, you will want to adapt them to fit your students purposes, your goals, your teaching style, and your working conditions. Where I have given examples of text or scenarios, it is always advisable that you substitute your own text or scenarios if doing so would more closely meet the needs of your group of students.

When considering the appropriateness of any given exercise for your class, consider the learning styles of your students. Some students are natural role players, and some can learn to be productive in role playing; yet, there are others for whom role playing and "artificial" situations have no validity as teaching tools. To some degree, students' feelings about the validity of teaching techniques are often self-fulfilling prophecies. For this reason, do not forget that the theater arts have more to offer than performing exercises. As you will see from this chapter, theatrical approaches can take on a number of forms. It is for you to choose the exercises that best suit the personalities of you and your students. Do not, however, interpret this to mean that students will only benefit from participation in familiar classroom exercises. Students are often delighted to be rescued from the "usual" by something which, to their delight, exploits their talents in a different way. Many of the exercises here can be used more than once. As students become accustomed to a way of working, they become more imaginative and productive in their participation.

Remember as you use these exercises that many of them include problem-solving sessions in which students must work in pairs or small groups and decide exactly how to go about accomplishing the tasks of the exercises. The strategies employed by the students during these creative brainstorming sessions are as important as the strategies employed while carrying out the tasks. Furthermore, many of these exercises involve the students as observers or members of the audience. Since, in any language or acting class, the actual time any given participant has to perform is only a fraction of the total time available, it is imperative that the students make productive use of the observation time. The classroom should be viewed as a performance laboratory in which students study the performances of classmates in order to discover strategies to employ and pitfalls to avoid.

It is impossible to dictate to our students what they should do or say in every situation they will encounter. Instead, it is desirable to give students a range of strategies to choose from as they communicate. The exercises in this chapter will help students become more flexible communicators and provide them with choices.

OBSERVATION

From day-to-day observations, an actor picks up characteristics which might be incorporated in a role. When building a single role, an actor might use the walk of a man he saw last week in a train station, the smile of a woman he talked to at a party, the hand wringing of a relative, the stuttering speech of a friend, and the piercing eye contact of a stranger in a restaurant.

Language learners (and others learning to communicate) should observe as carefully and imaginatively as does the actor. Observation prepares us to use our imagination to recognize and appreciate the messages encoded in the vast and complex systems of human behavior. Through observation, we discover new communication strategies that we can employ as we "negotiate" communication with others. We can observe in order to learn about the behavior of a particular individual, or the behavior of a group of people within a culture, subculture, or situation. We can also observe to broaden our experience and stimulate our imaginations in order to better understand how humans communicate.

As language learners, our students should develop the habit of looking for alternative reasons for human behavior and develop imaginations that will perceive behavior in people which might otherwise be missed. Experience in observation helps us to understand why we sometimes jump to conclusions that might be false or misleading simply because we have "seen" something. In addition, we can better understand the varied impressions different people might have of us in any given situation. In short, we can learn to perceive and understand a wider range of human behavior.

Observation Tasks

Use observation assignments and discussions to make students aware of opportunities they have to gather information about the target language and culture by developing and using their powers of observation. You can give students freedom in their observation tasks, letting them formulate their own categories and ways of classifying what they see. You can also guide them by telling them to observe specific elements of behavior. For example, instruct your students to use observation to study one or more of the items below.

walks

arm and hand gestures

facial expressions

sitting positions/standing positions

breathing movements and sounds

proxemics: seating space, standing space, talking space, passing space

eye contact

physical contact

people observing their environment

people who seem oblivious to their environment

people who know they are being watched

people who do not know they are being watched

people in specific relationships: parent/child, siblings, lovers, friends, colleagues, business associates, strangers, etc.

Class Discussions and Exercises

1. Class members report on observations they have made of the culture they are living in. Assign observations in advance, directing students to observe particular people, places, types of interactions, or characteristics. Discuss each observation using both logic and imagination to come up with possible explanations for the observed behavior. Discuss whether or not a particular observation is possible to interpret definitively, given the information available. Note the influences of the observer's background (culture) on the observation. (For reports on cultures which the learners are not presently living in, use photos, literature, the teacher's knowledge, and reports from those who have been there.)

2. Have learners incorporate actual observations made into a fictional character sketch (written, verbal, or performed) of the people involved. Include the known information and create missing details that would be consistent with the character.

   Example: A student reports:
   I was in a laundromat (U.S.A.) and saw a coin on the floor. Another customer also saw the coin, and I observed him cover the coin with his foot and then look around to see if anyone would claim it. No one noticed him (except me), so he picked up the coin and used it. I was surprised at his lack of boldness.

   POSSIBLE CHARACTER SKETCH: This fellow is a university student in his twenties. He probably has enough money, but enjoys the adventure of "discovering" unexpected money. He is probably basically honest so would feel embarrassed if he were to be caught using someone else's coin. He is also rational and knows that the true owner of the coin will never return to find it. Although he enjoys using the "free" coin, he would also be generous and let a friend use some of his laundry detergent, give his friend a ride in his car, buy his friend a cup of coffee, etc.

3. Use a picture to stimulate discussion. Find as many visual cues as possible to an interpretation of the characters in the picture. Examine clothing, posture, setting, action, etc. Again, use both logic and imagination to stimulate discussion.

4. Arrange chairs in a semicircle and have one student stand facing the class. As the student stands facing the class, have the classmates make a verbal list of the student's appearance. These observations should be both factual and interpretive: e.g., "His left arm is on his hip" (factual), or "He looks like he enjoys being watched by all of us" (interpretive). Point out the difference between objective and subjective observations.

5. List some cultural stereotypes on the board. Discuss the basis for these stereotypes. On what possible truths might they be based? Give evidence from actual observations. List alternative explanations. What falsehoods might they propagate? List alternatives.

6. Create some fictional circumstance surrounding a stereotypical person or situation. How would such a person behave? List possible alternative manifestations of this stereotypical behavior. Elicit reports of observations of behavior that deviate from the stereotype.

7. After role playing, scene performances, simulations, and other types of presentations, discuss observations made during the presentations. Have the class apply what they are learning about observation to in-class events. Don't regard the end of a presentation as being the end of the activity.

Using the Senses for Observation

Devote time to each of the five senses (seeing, hearing, smelling, tasting, touching) in isolation. In class, discuss sensations and experiences involving each sense. Tell students to spend time out of class using one sense at a time to observe. For example, from time to time, over a period of a few days, students might concentrate on whatever it is they are tasting. They should attempt to remember the sensations and then report back to the class, putting their observations *into words*. Below are suggestions to guide your observation assignments, but your students will probably need little help in coming up with interesting observations on which to report.

Taste

Language learners in a foreign culture will naturally notice the native food. Comparisons with food at home are inevitable and discussing these comparisons is a good way for learners to share information about their own cultures. In general, how do the tastes in the culture being studied compare with those of the students' native culture? Do they clash? Language learners often appreciate the opportunity to learn vocabulary that relates to the buying, cooking, and eating of food. Students learning about a culture in which they are not living can also learn a lot from the food of that culture. Although they are not living in the "foreign" culture, they can learn by reading, by hearing the reports of those who have been there, and best of all, by eating food characteristic of the culture. In addition, learners may notice things about taste sensations experienced by members of the culture being studied. Encourage them to discuss the implications of a culture's taste experiences for understanding that culture better. Learners might observe and talk about the influences of ethnic populations and natural resources on people's eating habits, as indicated by the concentration of certain ethnic restaurants and grocery stores, or the popularity of regional foods. Learners studying the

United States, for example, might notice Mexican food in Texas, gyros in Chicago, maple syrup in Vermont, and so forth. What can one say about the fact that many Americans seem to prefer fast food at lunch time to food that is more carefully prepared? Are Americans born with callous, unappreciative taste buds, or is their preference for fast food at lunch time more a reflection of attitudes like "time is money," and "business before pleasure"? What about people in other countries which also support a fast-food culture? Furthermore, can it be said that the existence of many fast-food restaurants precludes the existence of cultivated tastes in food?

Smell

Smelling, of course, relates to tasting. In an apartment building, one can often determine the neighbor's cooking preferences simply by walking down the hall. Smell also provides clues to the local industries. City dwellers become accustomed to different types of local pollution, and they learn to distinguish automobile pollution from local factory pollution. In addition, it is not difficult to distinguish a paper mill from a coffee processing plant. In rural areas, one can smell the nearby farms and sometimes know what kind they are. One's sense of smell can often tell one which way the wind is blowing. What does an ocean breeze smell like? What smells do the natives associate with seasons? What about the people themselves? How do they smell? Do they wear perfumes? When, where, and why? How do people in the United States, for example, associate social life and bad breath? Are advertisements for mouthwash and toothpaste to be believed? What is considered "good breath"? How do the natives feel about smoking and health? Is there a warning on cigarette packs? Which public places have no-smoking sections? Is this a law? Is it polite to smoke in other people's homes?

Touch

Climate is a primary concern to people visiting another country. Observe how climate influences clothing styles, architecture (why does California have more flat roofs than does Chicago?), social interaction (where do the sidewalk café sitters and beach combers go in the winter?), health, and even productivity. What kind of heating/air conditioning do the natives have in their homes, if any? What temperatures do they maintain in their homes? How else does the environment being observed "feel"? How do people sit when they eat: on the floor or in chairs? Do they sleep on mats or in beds with mattresses and box springs? What do they cover themselves with when they sleep?

What about touching other people? Where, how, and why do other people touch? Who touches whom? What messages are communicated through physical contact?

What about touching people's possessions? What is allowed? I have been chastised abroad for picking up fruit which I intended to buy. Because I didn't look first, I didn't notice that none of the other customers in the market were touching their purchases until the sellers handed them over. Careful pointing was the norm. In a separate incident, the wife of one of my students was arrested in a grocery store, on her first weekend in the United States, because she put some groceries in her handbag before paying for them. In her country, shoppers bring their own handbags to the market, and fill them as they shop. In addition, harsh penalties effectively eliminate shoplifting as a serious problem in her country. At home, her actions would hardly have made her a shoplifting suspect.

Don't forget to watch for patterns in proxemics. How close do people stand and move in relation to other people? How does eye "contact" change in relation to distance, situations, and personal relationships? Observe ways in which the eyes are used not only to "see" people, but also to contact or "touch" other people.

Hearing

What do your students discover through concentrated listening? Of course they should attune their ears to the language. How loud is it spoken? How are pronunciation and intonation used? Are dialects distinguishable? What do people actually say to other people? In addition to language sounds, what other sounds are there? What sorts of traffic sounds are there? Do the neighbors have noisy stereos, parties, or voices? What kinds of music do people prefer? Where do people listen to music? What is "muzak"? Is it played in so many public places (in the United States) because it is a national passion, or is it a privacy screen used to cover conversation? How do the natives react to foreign accents or foreign languages spoken in their presence? Direct students to radio and television programs of interest. Television programs captioned for the hearing impaired are also well suited for the language learner.

Instruct students to eavesdrop in public. Tell them to practice mimicry as often as possible. Encourage them to repeat (discreetly) words and sentences they overhear in passing, mimicking the sounds they hear.

Seeing

The eyes should always be busy gathering information. Encourage students to try to make inferences based on what they see, but warn them of making oversimplified or steadfast conclusions. "People watching" should be a way of life for language learners. Instruct them to watch for deviations and exceptions as well as patterns and norms. Have them recreate what they see through role playing, or by imitating a walk, posture, or gesture. Tell them to practice describing what they see by examining a subject, looking away and describing it, then taking a second look to check for accuracy and detail.

Watching for Movement Patterns

Have students observe different people going through the same situations. Tell them to watch for specific patterns that recur in many or all of the cases. Have them describe and discuss these patterns with the class. Why do the patterns observed occur repeatedly with different people? What do the gestures mean, if anything? A video recording of people in actual situations that reveals recurring patterns is useful for this exercise because sections of the tape can be viewed more than once during the discussion.

Examples

Watch people:

    a. enter the same room for a meeting

    b. enter a crowded restaurant and find places to sit

    c. enter a crowd of people who are standing and find a place to stand

    d. getting onto buses, trains, or planes

    e. walking down a hallway where there is a bulletin board that at least some of the people stop to read

    f. waiting for something or someone

    g. meeting people

    h. parting company

The Living Environment: Discussions and Exercises

In the target culture, what do the buildings and other man-made constructions look like? What building materials are used? Why? What are the functions or reasons for the designs? How does the appearance of man-made objects reflect climate, natural resources, local technology, aesthetic preferences, and living practices? Look at the inside of homes, offices, and other buildings. What can we learn from the furniture and its arrangement? In homes, for example, what are the functions of the various rooms?

In his book on Saudi Arabia called *The Kingdom*, Robert Lacey describes a low-cost housing development built in Saudi Arabia:

> No expense has been spared to accommodate the Saudi way of life: each apartment has separate reception rooms for male and female entertaining and extra bedrooms so that children of different sexes may sleep apart.

A contrast between living practices in some homes in Bogota, Colombia and the expectations of some American visitors to Bogota is described in Gordon's *Living in Latin America*. The American students were surprised to learn that the living room was not a central gathering place or an all-purpose room as in many American homes, but a special room reserved for receiving guests. This room was avoided at other times by the family members who did not wish to disturb the quiet orderliness of the room. Furthermore, an open-air connection between garage and living room made it possible for guests to see the finely polished family automobile—a status symbol—which was encased in a clean, eye-appealing garage with a clean tiled floor. The Colombian garage is a contrast to the greasy-floored American garage, which is often a holding area for garbage receptacles and family junk, as well as the family car (if indeed there is any space remaining for the car).

Exercises

1. Have students draw plans of typical homes in their countries, and explain the functions of the various sections of the homes. How is territoriality manifested in the home? Who does what, where? Are doors kept open or shut? Locked or unlocked? Examine differences. Compare with the target culture.

   Taking one room at a time, have students describe the environment in the home. Ask them, for example, to recall everything they can about their living room. What is done there and what are its physical characteristics? If possible, pass around magazines with pictures of homes in both the native and target cultures.

2. Have volunteers simulate specific situations in homes, for example, greeting guests at one's home, seating guests at one's dinner table, asking someone if it is "okay" to enter a specific room, drinking tea in one's own kitchen vs. drinking tea in a friend's living room, etc.

3. Break the class into pairs to create short, realistic interactions that indicate specific locations. Actors should not give the locations away through direct explanation, but should show the audience, through actions, where the interactions take place. Allow five to ten minutes of preparation time the first time or two, then try more spontaneous interactions with only short preparation time. Actors should remember that because of differing cultural perspectives, a given action may suggest one location to some people and a different location to others.

On Location

Give students a list of suggested places to visit in order to observe people. With or without a follow-up classroom discussion, such observation experiences broaden students' perspectives on the target culture and language simply because they are different from the experiences the students have on a daily basis. Students reporting interesting observations to the class inform classmates about the existence of these opportunities. The list below is only an example. You can create your own to serve the needs of your students and exploit the opportunities that exist in your area. Remember to include places that students would not visit on their own.

Places to Visit (Instructions to Learners):

1. Go to a place where people wait in lines (especially several lines at once), e.g., fast-food places at lunchtime, banks during busy hours, the post office during busy hours, bus and train stations, supermarkets, airports, theaters, cinemas, sports events, etc. Observe how people negotiate territory in the lines, where they look, whom they talk to, and other aspects of their line-waiting behavior.

2. Ride on public transportation in an area where you don't normally ride. Observe the interaction, or lack thereof, of the people. How much, how loud, and with whom do they talk? How do people negotiate space and lay claims to seats?

3. If you have to wait in an office where there are several employees, observe how the employees interact with each other. How much do they talk to each other and about what? If possible, compare the interactions of fellow employees who are talking about matters relating to their jobs and those relating to other things, such as social life.

4. Go to an elementary school when children are coming, going, or at recess, and watch them. How do their interactions differ from those of children in your native country?

5. When you are in a bar or restaurant, try to characterize the clientele. Compare the customers in different establishments.

6. If there are low-income areas in your city, and you are not located in one, go to such an area. What is the housing like? Is there government subsidized housing? What does it look like? Are mass transportation systems evident? Observe school children in one of these areas. What kind of businesses do you see, if any? What is for sale in the stores? Find a place where people interact in public and observe the people. Are there differences in their behavior and language that you can describe?

7. Go to an all-night diner at 2 A.M. and watch the people who come in. How would you describe them? Where are they coming from, and where do you think they are going? What do they eat?

8. Go to a place where people are carrying newspapers or buying them. Watch for example, people who are traveling to and from work. Is it possible to generalize as to what "types" of people buy which newspapers? Are there differences?

9. Go to the local unemployment office and sit down near the people who are waiting in line. What types of people are there? What do they talk about, if anything? How many of them are there? How long does each person stay at the office?

10. Visit a variety of places where employees, or people of the same profession, gather to eat, drink, or socialize; for example, bars after working hours, restaurants at lunch hours, a truck stop on or near a highway (sit at the counter if there appear to be truck drivers sitting there too). Notice the different ways of interacting.

11. Go to a place where families are gathered, for example, the local swimming pool, picnic area, or school event. Observe family interaction. Note the similarities and differences in roles "across families," i.e., watch all of the fathers, then all of the mothers, then all of the older children, and so forth.

A Questionnaire

The questionnaire below is an exercise involving reading, writing, and reflection. Use it to help students examine roles in interaction. Discussion should follow. Change questions and add new ones to suit your purposes.

Interaction Questionnaire

Think of an interaction you have had recently. Use the questionnaire to analyze the interaction.

1. Briefly describe the situation.
2. Give location of interaction.
3. Note time.
4. To whom did you talk?
5. What was that person's role in relation to you as you saw it?
6. As he/she saw it (in your opinion)?
7. What was your role in relation to him/her as you saw it?
8. As he/she saw it?
9. Did he/she fulfill your expectations of him/her?   Yes.   No.   Why? Why not?
10. Did you fulfill his/her expectations of you?   Yes.   No.   I don't know.   Why?   Why not?
11. What did you want from this interaction?
12. What did he/she want?
13. Did you have any problems understanding each other? Explain.
14. If yes, then were these problems resolved?
15. How were you misunderstood? Why?
16. Describe the physical language of the interaction (yours and his/hers).
17. Describe standing or sitting posture.

18. Describe hand gestures.
19. What was the degree of relaxation/tension? How was this manifested?
20. Describe facial expressions.
21. Describe eye focus (length and placement of eye contact).
22. Did the other person move in relation to you?
23. What did these movements communicate to you?
24. How did you move?
25. What might your movements have communicated to him/her?
26. Why did you move as you did?
27. Were there any gestures or words used that you consider inappropriate?
28. What moods were you and he/she in?
29. Was your voice loud enough? Too loud?
30. What about his/her voice?
31. Is there anything you wish you had said or done?
32. Was there anything you did not know how to express?
33. What could have been done to make this interaction smoother and more comfortable, or to improve the communication that took place?
34. Other comments, observations.

CHARACTER STUDY

Advising

Students work in groups of two or three to make a list of recommendations for the benefit of people who will soon be having a given experience. Choose experiences that the students have actually had and ask them to put themselves in the shoes of people who have never had the experiences. The students should try to recall their "first time." Experiences to choose from (for example):

1. Students going through Customs in order to study in this country.
2. Students preparing to study at a foreign university.
3. Students living with, dining with, spending some time with, a host family.
4. Tourists visiting a particular city.

Students take time to assemble recommendations in writing. Then a spokesperson from each group presents the recommendations to the class. The class makes changes (additions, criticisms, etc.) which the team notes. The teams then meet to write up a final report, which the teacher collects.

Substitution and Recall

This exercise encourages the use of substitution and recall as aids to understanding the unfamiliar circumstances of others. Choose a short article about a person. A sample is shown on page 61. Have students read and discuss the article. I often allow students to discuss articles in groups so that they can supply each other with vocabulary definitions and explanations. (You could also take a character from a listening comprehension passage or an oral anecdote.) Then have the students answer the questions below. The answers can be presented by the students orally from notes they write for themselves; or the answers could be recorded as a writing assignment that you could collect. In either case, allow students to present answers orally and encourage discussion. The discussion facilitates ensemble building since students reveal a bit of themselves as they report. Before starting the exercise, introduce the students to the concepts of substitution and recall (see Chapter 2).

Instructions to Students:

Imagine that you are going to play the role of the character in the story. In building your character, you will use recall and substitution.

Step I: List five experiences which you have not had, but which your character has had, and which you would need to understand in order to play the character.

GENERAL

Search for Mark Thatcher in Sahara

A full-scale search was going on in the Sahara last night for the Prime Minister's son Mark Thatcher and his rally crew who were reported stranded in southern Algeria after their car broke down four days ago.

Earlier reports that he had been found were denied and the organisers of the 10,000 mile Paris-Dakar rally were said to be very concerned for the safety of Mark and his co-driver Charlotte Verney of France.

The Prime Minister was said last night to be very worried " but not panicking . . . because he may well turn up within five minutes."

From: *The Financial Times* (of London)

Jan. 13, 1982

Sample answers for Mark Thatcher.

1. He is the son of Britain's Prime Minister. My family is not famous.
2. I have never been in a desert.
3. I have never been lost in a wilderness.
4. I have no interest in sports that involve cars.
5. I don't know anything about his co-driver, other than the few facts given in the article.

Step II: For each experience listed above, suggest how you might use substitution and/or recall to compensate for the fact that you are not really Mark Thatcher.

Sample answers.

1. Mark Thatcher can count on the fact that his family is famous and therefore public attention will be focused on his plight and cause a search party to be launched. I can imagine that some institution that does care about me has the money, influence and power to implement a wide-scale search for me, as if I were the son of a public figure. For example, my family, school, friends, government, rally sponsors, or fellow car rally enthusiasts might be able to cause a search party to be launched.

2. I know enough about the desert to imagine it. I can recall extremely hot summers and cold winters and the need I sometimes have to protect myself from the elements. I can substitute my impressions of the vastness of the sea because I have been offshore in boats. I have also been camping in a very large forest and can recall the feeling of being one of the only humans within a vast area.

3. I have been lost for hours in a big city and although the situation was only temporary, it was very frustrating. I also remember depending on my car for warmth once when I was lost in the country during a winter snow storm.

4. I do like other sports, and like my character, I don't mind the "risks" when I participate in them. I like water sports for example, and know how to do them safely. I have friends who are car buffs as well, so I can recall their enthusiasm toward the sport.

5. Although I don't know the woman he is with, I imagine that she is most likely a friend. At least one common interest they have is an interest in car rallies. She would probably be someone he enjoys being with, and someone who is a good team member in his opinion. She might be a romantic interest of his. I can recall a variety of people I have known who I can combine in my mind as a substitute for her.

A Writing Exercise

It is a simple matter to incorporate character study or study of culture into a writing exercise. Any cultural topic relevant to your students' interests can be roughly summarized by you in the form of notes and then converted by the students into an essay or report. I have done this below with the American education system. Make comparisons to the education systems in other countries using your students as sources of information. Finally, have students use the notes to write a short report on the American education system. The same exercise could be used to teach students about the American government, American cities, transportation in the United States, holidays in the United States, what the natives do with their leisure time, sources of news (newspapers, radio, television, etc.) in City X (choose one), and so forth. Of course any other country can be examined in this way as well. Especially interesting would be the language learners' own countries.

Example: Below are basic details of the American education system.

starting age: 5 or 6

kindergarten (optional)

elementary school = grades 1–6 (sometimes 1–5)

junior high school = grades 7–9 (sometimes 6–8)

high school = grades 9–12

school mandatory until age 16

average age at high school graduation: 18

requirements for university entrance: acceptable grade point average (GPA)

university degrees: bachelor's — 4 years
master's — 1–2 years
doctorate — 3–5 years (required for university professors)

Notes: Most students graduate from high school. A large percentage attend colleges and universities. Many college graduates get advanced degrees, i.e., master's and doctorates.

Music Matching

Give the class three character profiles or descriptions and listen to three or more songs. Break the class into groups. Each group should read the character descriptions and decide which descriptions go with which songs. The class then reassembles and reports results. Each group must have summarized reasons (spoken or written) for matching songs with characters as they did.

Differences in matching should be justified and debated if necessary. Matches can be made for either obvious or abstract reasons.

This exercise can be repeated using increasingly less obvious matches, leaving the matching more open to interpretation each time.

Option: The character sketches can be replaced by scenes or stories from fiction, newspapers, or even anecdotes related by class members in a story-telling session.

Option: One scene or story is read by the class. Then, a series of songs is played, with lyrics supplied in writing if necessary. The class reviews five to ten songs and chooses one for each character. More songs should be used than there are characters so that only some will be chosen. This task resembles that which directors face when choosing background music for a stage play or film.

Matching Example

The character sketches below can be matched with the songs, "Streets of London" (Ralph McTell), "Why Can't the English" (from *My Fair Lady* by Alan Jay Lerner and Frederick Loewe), and "In My Life" (Lennon and McCartney).

THE STUDENTS: A group of students have lived together for two years at a university. These men and women are close friends who have shared both good times and bad over the past two years. Some of them have even had romances. Now that they have graduated, they are all moving to different places. They will be starting different occupations as well. Although they have been good friends for two years, they might not ever see each other again. As they move their belongings out of the house on their last day together, they look forward to their future. They are sorry to be splitting up, but for them, it is a regular part of life. They will always be on the move.

THE SPEAKER: An English speaker named Earl is irritated by a friend who tells him that he mispronounced the word "car." The friend told him that he should not forget to pronounce the r sound in "car." Earl, however, never pronounces the r; he says "car" with a silent r. Furthermore, Earl's friend is always correcting his pronunciation in public. Earl has been speaking English all of his life, and he doesn't like to be told how to pronounce it. Earl's wife thinks he is silly to get so irritated over such a little thing. She tells him not to get so upset when his friend corrects his language. She says the friend is just kidding him.

JANE: Jane is a social worker. She feels a great compassion for the down-and-out. She spends much of her time working at several of the shelters that operate in the city, where the poor can find a place to sleep and a hot meal.

She is naturally quite aware of the many problems that face the poor, and she knows that they are not easily solved. Sometimes she gets angry when she hears people complain about how hard life is. She feels that most people don't really have a hard life, and that the ones who do, usually aren't the ones who complain.

Deciphering and Interpreting Songs

Exercise 1: Each student brings in a recording of a song in English, plays it, and gives a prepared interpretation of the lyrics. The teacher and fellow students supply vocabulary for describing musical styles and interpreting lyrics when necessary.

This is a good ensemble-building exercise. Classmates are able to express aspects of their personalities through their choice of music and interpretation. Students' attention is also focused on the music of the local culture.

Because all students might not have records or tapes at home, access to a language laboratory and tapes should be offered if possible. Students might be willing to supply their own tapes for other students to use if necessary. Encourage students to enlist the aid of a native speaker, when available, for interpreting slang.

Exercise 2: The actual transcribing of lyrics can be done in groups and in class. Many heads are sometimes better than one—especially when lingo and slang are involved. Done orally as a group, this should not be a painstaking process. Discuss relevant background and cultural information needed to understand each song.

Exercise 3: Give students lyrics to a song, but with words deleted as in a cloze passage (say, every seventh word). Play the song several times, letting students fill in their papers individually. Then review the passage as a class. Discuss meaning and interpretation.

Cartoons

Using cartoons, students can learn about the natives through their humor and satire. What do your students need to know before they can appreciate the point of the cartoon below? If one must explain a joke or cartoon in order for students to appreciate it, the humor may be lost in the process, but the students will gain insight into the point of view of the natives for whom the cartoon was written.

Watch papers and magazines for cartoons that you can use in class to make points about language and culture. Have students do the same. Also have students bring in cartoons from their native languages to explain to the class.

Some Questons to Ask

Is the cartoon funny? Why? To whom is it funny? Who is the audience? Is it political? Sarcastic? Symbolic? Who are the characters? What is the setting? What current events or situations compose the background of this cartoon?

DOONESBURY   **by Garry Trudeau**

Role Playing

Once students understand the characters in a cartoon, you can use the cartoon as a springboard for a role-playing exercise. Break students into groups so that each group contains the number of people that there are in the cartoon. In the case of the Doonesbury cartoon above, students will break into pairs. Give them five to fifteen minutes to think of a situation in which these characters might find themselves and create a conversation illustrating the situation. Reassemble the class and have each group perform the conversation. The performance need not be based on a written or memorized script. It can be improvised.

The Press

What can we learn about a culture from its press, radio and television? The following exercises will introduce learners to what is available locally in terms of mass media, and help give them a perspective from which to evaluate and compare the various offerings.

1. As a class, list the newspapers read by members of the target culture. Try to describe the newspapers in terms of good vs. bad journalism. Try to place each paper on a political continuum from left to right. Find other means of classification. Instruct students to examine papers over a period of a week in search of evidence to support (or refute) the above descriptions.

2. In groups, examine two or more newspapers of the same day. Compare and contrast the papers using articles from each to support the group's comparisons. Be sure to note the "look" of each paper (type of print used, pictures, sensational headlines), as well as the content. Later, present group findings to class.

3. As a class, list the types of entertainment and information offered by television and radio in the area. What do the natives prefer to watch/listen to? What types of programs are missing? What sources of information are available that list daily programming for radio and television?

4. Discuss how the mass media in the United States (or any other country) is used to communicate locally, nationally, and internationally. How does advertising affect the public? For example, how does the American media affect what Americans and others know about the world? How is the media used during an election campaign? What defenses do the members of a culture, which is so heavily influenced by mass media, develop to defend themselves against misinformation?

5. Instruct students to look for articles in newspapers that reinforce stereotypical views of a culture or group of people. They can present articles or excerpts for discussion.

Give an example of such an article to the class to use in a group reading/discussion assignment. Working in groups of three or four, have students try to find sentences in the article that make sweeping generalizations about people. Reassemble the class and compare group findings. Then, have students work in groups again, to rewrite the most obviously oversimplified statements, making them either more truthful, or at least less general and less absolute.

Below is an example of the type of article that can be used for Exercise 5.

DAILY EXPRESS Thursday January 14 1982

ANTHEA DISNEY
IN NEW YORK

THE most overworked word yet introduced to the American vocabulary is
"gourmet." Restaurants, thriving food
boutiques, and now even speciality
departments in supermarkets are
attracting customers in their millions
with the implicit promise of belonging
to the culinary cognoscenti.

Traditionally Americans knew and cared
little for food. As long as it was whole-
some and filled them up, they were
happy.

Next came the love affair with junk food.
As long as it was quick and filled them
up, they were happy.

But in the past few years a revulsion
against the nation's eating habits has
grown up, based on urban America's
growing sophistication and the mortifying
discovery that the rest of the world con-
siders them gastronomic savages.

But, as with every other fad, people here
have gone over the top in their anxiety
to reform. The new maxim seems to be :
If a little is good, more is better.

From: *Daily Express* (of London) *Jan. 14, 1982.*

The Media: A Group Project

This project should follow discussion of the media as described in the previous exercises. The time required depends on the length of the articles you use; you could use more than one class period.

In this exercise students put themselves into the shoes of news gatherers, copy editors, and readers of newspapers.

Procedure

Divide the class into groups of three or four students.

Step 1: Groups meet to decide what type of newspaper they are going to represent, i.e., who are the readers? Readers should be defined in terms of age, education, geographic location, lifestyle, political leanings (if any), reading ability, interests, etc. This decision will affect the writing and reporting styles.

Step 2: Each group summarizes its decisions briefly on paper, and presents this to the teacher. The teacher gives each group a news event. (*Options*: If all groups work on the same event, then comparisons can be made in the discussion of how well the event was handled by the groups. If each group works on a different event, then a greater variety of news can be dealt with in discussion.)

Step 3: Groups meet to decide how to gather the news, e.g., where in the world to send reporters, who to interview, and what type of information they will seek. These decisions are summarized on paper and given to the teacher.

Step 4: Upon receiving the summary from Step 3, the teacher gives each group a pile of articles, newspapers, and magazines which include reports on the event named in Step 2. Groups meet to research the story. Articles are chosen from the pool of information to be used as information sources. Group members can distribute the articles for reading or tackle each article as a group. (This depends on the time and the reading abilities within the group.) Members extract relevant information from the articles to be used in the group article. The group should search especially for information that will fulfill the objectives established in Steps 1 and 3. The group then decides which "facts" will be used in the group article. The group then writes an article that reports on the event. Sources should be quoted. (See language sample below.)

Step 5: The teacher edits the articles and makes copies for the class.

Step 6: The class reassembles and reads the articles (or hears each one read by a member of the appropriate group).

Discuss how well each group achieved the goals they set down in Steps 1 and 3. How appropriately was the chosen audience addressed? Were the sources quoted properly? Would the sources quoted be credible to the chosen audience? How well is the situation summarized? What about the writing itself? Review language points.

Language for Quoting Media Sources

The list below (or a similar list) could be given to the students to expose them to the types of sentences used in the media to name sources. The list will help make them *aware* of the function of such sentences when they read or listen to news reports, and it will help them write their own reports.

In an interview with _____, Mr. X said . . .

A reliable source was reported to have said . . .

A spokeswoman for X said . . .

An article in the *National Enquirer* reported him to have said . . .

A photograph in *The New York Times* showed Mr. X _____ing . . . in _____.

Sources close to the President . . . told reporters that . . .

It is believed that . . .

The *Tribune* reported . . .

. . . a top government official said here Monday.

The reports were based on remarks attributed to . . .

City officials are reported to have . . .

The *Daily News* quoted him as saying . . .

THE VOICE

First Impressions: Personality, Tone of Voice, and Appearance

Use video to help students think about how the sound of a person's voice influences one's impression of that person. Use a short segment (five minutes) of an interview or any recording of normal speaking voices. Follow this procedure:

1. First, have the class listen to the segment without looking at the picture.

2. Then, have them think about the person connected with the voice. Give everyone time to think and to write a few notes describing impressions of the speaker.

3. Next, have the class discuss their impressions. Ask learners to make guesses as to the physical appearance of the speaker.

4. After the discussion, listen to the segment again while viewing the picture.

5. Finally, discuss impressions including comments on how well initial impressions matched up with final impressions.

Speaking About Voices

What makes one speaker's English different from another's? To get students in the habit of listening for differences in the sound of English-speaking voices, play recordings of two different speakers and ask students to contrast and compare the speakers' voices. If you are able to use video, include discussion of the visual impressions made by the speakers. Use the following questions and your own.

1. Does either speaker sound more educated, upperclass, superior, approachable, distant, defensive, confident, intelligent, trustworthy, naive, warm, or cold?
2. What makes the speakers' voices sound different?
3. Who makes vowels "broader," (i.e., of longer duration, more drawn out)?
4. Who is more specific with consonants?
5. Whose intonation range is greater? Whose voice is generally higher? Generally lower?
6. Who speaks fastest?
7. Who speaks louder? Softer?
8. Who moves his/her mouth more?
9. Whose voice sounds more nasal?
10. Who is easier to understand? Why?
11. Can you tell what part of the country/world these people are from?
12. How would you describe the sound of their dialect? For each speaker complete the following:

    Vowels are _____

    Consonants are _____

    Stress is _____

    Intonation is _____

    Volume is _____

    Rate of speech is _____

Vocal Warm-ups and Exercises

This section does not cover everything you need to teach about pronunciation. Rather, it contains suggestions of how you can insert techniques from the theater into pronunciation work. The techniques suggested here should make the learning of pronunciation a more effective process. If there were some easy, quick method for making people flexible enough to change vocal habits quickly and radically, it would probably have been discovered long ago. The fact is that vocal flexibility is the result of experience, lots of practice, and attention to many small, but important, factors that many people are not aware of or do not care about. Posture is one. Breathing is another. Breathing and posture are related. If we have good posture, our breathing is easier. If our breathing is more under control, then so are our voices.

I use vocal warm-ups similar to those used in choral and drama rehearsals. These warm-ups can be used in many language lessons, but are especially appropriate for pronunciation lessons, or when vocal production is being emphasized. The logic is simple: we should not expect students to make great strides in producing strange and challenging new sounds (English sounds) without first warming-up and learning to skillfully use their vocal apparatuses, any more than we would expect a person to run two miles without first warming up and conditioning the muscles involved. Vocal warm-up sessions focus students' attention on their vocal apparatuses (awareness is half the battle), and the students get "tuned" as an ensemble as they begin listening to each other. Finally, these warm-ups teach students about how their voices work.

If you have never used vocal warm-ups like these, I suggest you practice them on friendly test subjects (fellow teachers, for example) before trying them on your classes. To "conduct" these exercises, you do not need a singing voice or musical training. It is helpful, however, if you have never seen a conductor warm-up a choir, to try to visit some choral rehearsals, as this would increase your appreciation for these exercises.

When leading vocal warm-ups, an active, lively tempo should be maintained. Students will follow your tempo if you use short clear orders illustrated by your own actions. Use brief commands like: "breathe," "say _____," "do this," "repeat," "again," "feel the vibrations," "feel them here," "now, feel them here," and so forth. Clear, confident instructions are necessary. As the students are warming up, be on the lookout for opportunities to suggest, correct, and compliment.

Encourage students to stand up straight when doing vocal warm-ups. Posture is important. Relaxation is too. Before embarking on a series of pronunciation exercises, have students stand and let their arms hang loosely at their sides. This is a minimum of posture education. The body is the instrument we use to produce vocal sounds. How we "hold" that instrument influences the sounds we are able to make. We do not want to restructure the posture of our students, and, of course, we cannot do that. We can, however, make them aware that their bodies are part of their vocal instruments. When they breathe, they should do so easily and efficiently. During many of these warm-ups, breathing should be a conscious activity. When the air space is filled, there should be a feeling that it is filling from the bottom up. The shoulders and stomach should not be actively engaged in the process of inhaling and exhaling; if they are, then there is wasted energy, or tension. It is the outgoing air that produces sound. It is important that we do not allow tension to interfere with the inhaling of air. In addition, it is in a relaxed state that we are most likely to be able to appreciate the effect various resonating areas have on the quality of the sound we produce.

The following warm-up exercises are meant to be done in sequence, but you can also use them a few at a time. They are intended to be used more than once with any given group of students. The first time through, you will have to teach the exercises to your students. In subsequent lessons you can move speedily through them.

Warm-ups

1. Close mouths. Make the space inside the mouth as big as possible without opening the lips. Don't bloat the cheeks with air. Remain as relaxed as possible. Next, open the mouth and move the lower jaw from side to side. Maintain a relaxed feeling.

   Next, without making a sound, go through the motions, in slow motion, of a big yawn. Repeat, and add sound.

   Then, close the eyes and "scrunch" (contract) the face making it as small as possible. Next, open the eyes and the face making it as large as possible. Repeat several times.

2. Breathe (slowly and deeply, filling the air space). Exhale. Repeat several times in unison. (Hereafter, each step begins with a deep breath. This is relaxing, and it encourages awareness of breath control. Without breath control, there is no voice control.)

3. Inhale (the command I use for this is "breathe"), and say, "mmmmmmmmmmmmm," with falling intonation. Begin at the top of your pitch range and slide down to the bottom. Remain relaxed. Take your time. Use the complete breath. Stay in unison. Repeat five or more times. Remember to breathe at the start of each. Ask the class to *feel* the vibrations caused by the high, medium, and low sounds. Ask them where they feel each sound. Recommend that they attempt to "place" the vibrations so that they are felt on the face next to the nose, on the roof of the mouth, on the forehead, and on the front teeth. (Students should try to minimize vibrations in the throat.) Remind them, often, to notice the feeling of the vibrations they make when they speak. These sensations can be controlled and manipulated to enhance the tone and clarity of vocal production.

4. Repeat step 3, but start low, go high, and fall to low again.

5. Inhale. Begin again at the high end of your pitch range saying "mmmmm" with falling intonation. After you have begun the de-

scent, open your lips so that the sound changes from "mmmmm" to the vowel sound /ä/ as in father. Repeat this several times, and then do it with other vowels especially /ō/ as in no, /ē/ as in me, /ü/ as in blue, and /ā/ as in mate.

Remember to remain relaxed, take your time, and use a complete breath each time you slide from the top to the bottom of your range.

Encourage the participants to open directly to the vowel sound without adding other vowels or impure sounds in between the "mmm" and the vowel. Instruct participants to notice the difference in the feelings of the various vowels when doing this exercise. Tell them to note, for example, the location of the vibrations felt when producing the different sounds.

Continue this exercise until the feeling is relaxed and the changes in sound are easy to control.

This exercise might be visualized as follows:

```
M                              M
 M                              M
  M                              M
   M                              M
    M                              M
     M                              M
      M                              M
       a                              M
        a                              O
1. (Repeat    a                         O
   several times.)  a    2. (Change vowels.)  O
                 a                            O
                  a
```

6. Breathe deeply and say,

```
              imm
                 m
                  m
                   m
"vvvvvvvvvvvvvvvvv     m mmmmmmmmmmmmmmmmmm."
```
(Levels indicate intonation.) Repeat the above several times. Insist on a well-produced and sustained /v/. Ask students to tell where they feel the vibrations. From where to where do the vibrations move?

7. Inhale. Say, "/ä/ (as in *father*); this is the widest lip opening used in this exercise. Then, while sustaining the sounds, close the lips until the /ü/ (as in *blue*) sound is formed; this is the smallest lip opening used in this exercise. Repeat several times. Notice that the lips move through the positions of other vowel sounds as they move from /ä/ to /ü/. Notice, too, that the teeth should not need to be clamped together in order to move from the /ä/ to the /ü/. In other words, the resonating chamber inside the mouth should remain spacious no matter which vowel sound is being produced. Also, try moving from /ä/ to /ō/ (as in *no*), and from /ä/ to other vowels.

8. Breathe. Start on a sustained /ng/ and open to a vowel. Upon opening, let the intonation fall.

For example:

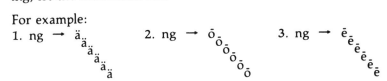

Repeat with other vowels. Repeat each attempt until students open to pure vowel sounds, i.e., no other vowel sounds should emerge between the /ng/ and the vowel sound.

9. Produce an exaggerated form of the word "wide" as follows. Start on a sustained /ü/ (as in *blue*), and open to a sustained /ä/ (as in *father*). From there, move to a sustained /ē/ (as in *tree*), and end with a plosive /d/.

   The leader should maintain an ensemble unison so that everyone makes the changes in sound and the plosive /d/ at the same time. This requires watching and listening to the leader.

   For example:

   üüüüüwäääääeeeeeed

(Repeat several times.)

10. Recite the following six lines, maintaining a rhythmic unison. Start slowly and speed up. The vowel sound is /ə/.

    1. pa pa pa
    2. ba ba ba
    3. ta ta ta
    4. da da da
    5. ka ka ka
    6. ga ga ga

    To teach the sequence, repeat two lines, slowly, until familiar. Then, put all six lines together. Insist on clear distinctions between the sounds. As in all of these exercises, pay particular attention to the sounds that your students do not have in their native languages. Without vocabulary, grammar, and communication to concern them, students should take advantage of the opportunity to focus their efforts on the accurate production of these sounds. Tell them to focus their attention on the *feeling* of the sounds.

11. Repeat a few select words exaggerating and controlling the articulation of the various sounds. For example, the words "meat and potatoes" would be repeated five to ten times. During the repetition, which sounds like a chant, the class would sustain the /m/, the /ē/,

the /ō/, and the /z/. The /t/, the /d/, and the /p/ would be carefully and clearly exploded. The teacher sets a tempo and the class maintains it. The result is an exaggerated pronunciation of the words. The object is to manipulate the articulating mechanisms.

12. Chant individual words exploding the plosives and stressing the major stressed syllable in an exaggerated fashion. A strict unison should be maintained. The dynamic focus of this exercise should be "staccato," (short, sharp sounds). Examples (repeat one at a time): "Nebraska," "Chicago."

13. Spell "Mississippi" quickly at least five times in rapid succession pronouncing each letter carefully and specifically. The sounds should be controlled. Start slowly and build up speed.

14. Take a deep breath, then, forcibly expel most of it in a short, sharp "Ha!" Repeat several times. Then, do the same with three Ha's for each breath. A gentle push should be felt down below the chest when the air is expelled. The sound should be powerful, but the feeling relaxed.

15. Blow air out through the lips causing them to flutter. Repeat at least six times.

16. Take a deep breath, then let it out with an explosive "blaaaaaaaaaaa" (/ă/ as in cat). Repeat at least three times.

Projecting the Voice

Occasionally, I have students who do not speak English loud enough. Appropriate volume levels differ across cultures. In American culture, a voice that carries can be an asset. A voice that does not carry can be an impediment to communication. I use the following exercises to demonstrate the use of breathing in projecting the voice.

Exercise

First, warm up the students' voices. Include the "Ha" warm-up. (See vocal warm-ups and exercises, #14.) Write a short dialogue on the board. See example below.

Stand students on opposite sides of the room in two lines facing each other. Use the same principle as in the "Ha" warm-up to project the lines, i.e., the lines should be "projected" using the diaphragm to push the air out. (Remember, this push should be powerful, but relaxed.) Instruct students to feel the air being controlled from below the chest, and to feel the resonation in the head and chest. Tell them to "fill the room with sound," and to try to "bounce the sound off the opposite wall." The bigger the room is, the better. Have the two groups call the dialogue in loud, but relaxed voices. Give one part of the dialogue to each group. Coach them to be louder as the dialogue progresses. Each line should be louder than the line before it.

Next, go down each line, giving each student a chance to read the dialogue with a student across the room. Allow students who have trouble projecting their voices several attempts. Encourage them to feel the resonation and allow the air flow to assist them. Caution all students as often as necessary to avoid forcing the voice to project. Relaxed proper use of the voice should suffice, but this may take practice.

Dialogue for Projection

1. Hey!
2. What?
1. Are you ready?
2. What?
1. Are you ready?
2. I can't hear you!
1. Let's get going. We'll be late!
2. In a minute! I'm not ready yet!
1. What?

Intonation without Words

Intonation sometimes communicates more than words. Acting courses or workshops often include some sort of exercise in which students communicate using intonation, but no words. Below are two examples.

1. Give the class a selection of short dialogues, scenes, poems, stories, or situations to act out. Students work in pairs. Each pair chooses one of the pieces and practices it aloud using intonation, but no words. The class then reassembles. Each pair performs its piece for the class. The audience should be able to determine which of the pieces is being performed.

2. Same as above except each pair sees only the piece which it is to perform. Without the aid of a written text, the audience must try to interpret each scene upon seeing it performed. The actors will find that their intended messages are not always accurately perceived by their audience.

Rhythm

Language learners should be made aware of the role rhythm plays in communication. Rhythm plays an important role as a medium of expression in language. When communicating, it is not only important to be able to interpret the rhythms one hears, but also to be able to control the rhythms one produces. This involves the coordination of mind and body in action. For the language speaker, like the musician playing an instrument, control of rhythms involves physical action as well as mental activity. The musician knows that rhythm can be felt as well as heard, and that the body can be taught to react to the feelings of rhythm as well as the sounds. A sense of rhythm can be heightened through awareness and practice.

The clapping of hands is like the playing of an instrument. Using the body as the instrument assures that the players will feel the rhythms as well as hear them.

Exercises

1. Record yourself clapping out a series of alternating rhythms. Leave space between phrases so that the students have time to mimic each phrase. Gradually lengthen the phrases so that students must reproduce increasingly longer rhythm patterns. Play the tape, and have students respond to each phrase by reproducing the rhythm in hand claps. The goal of the group should be to reproduce the taped phrases, clapping *in unison*. They should use the taped claps to set the tempo of their responses, leaving one beat between each phrase and the response. Start with phrases of about five beats in length.

2. Teach the students the words and rhythm to a familiar song. If you can find a song that everyone already knows, all the better. Have students say the words in rhythm. At this point, don't include the pitches (the tune). Next, have them clap the rhythm in unison. Work until the group can clap the entire song in unison.

3. *Clapping alternating stress*: Include the following clapping exercise in lessons on the alternating stress pattern. Students simply repeat the clapped pattern which you present. A continuous clapping dialogue is set up between teacher and students. Students should clap in unison. Each phrase consists of five claps. Alternate the major and minor stress patterns from phrase to phrase. You might, for example, clap the following pattern:

$$\overset{/}{1}\overset{/}{2}345 \quad \overset{/}{1}\overset{/}{2}345 \quad \overset{/}{1}\overset{/}{2}345 \quad \overset{/}{1}\overset{/}{2}345 \quad \overset{//}{1}2345$$

$$\overset{/}{1}\overset{//}{2}345 \quad \overset{///}{1}2345 \quad \overset{/}{1}\overset{//}{2}345 \quad \overset{///}{1}2345 \quad \overset{/}{1}234\overset{/}{5}$$

4. *Pass the poem (rhythm)*: Give students the text of a poem (or the verse of a song as in the case below) that depends on rhythm.

Example:

He's telling a terrible story
But it doesn't diminish his glory
For they would have taken his daughters
Over the billowy waters.
If he hadn't in elegant diction
Indulged in an innocent fiction
Which is not in the same category
As telling a regular terrible story.

(From *The Pirates of Penzance*, by Gilbert and Sullivan)

Have the class repeat the poem (or verse) aloud, in unison, until it is familiar, and the natural rhythm is established.

Then, (sitting in a circle, if possible) have the class recite the poem one person at a time, with each person reciting one or two lines. The speaking turn is passed around the circle. Practice until the rhythm of the poem is unbroken by unnatural pauses or inconsistent tempos from the students. (This is easier said than done.)

Next, pass the poem again, but instead of passing the turn clockwise or in a circular fashion, pass it through eye contact, i.e., each person reciting must make eye contact with another person, who then becomes the next speaker. Everyone must, of course, be looking at each speaker in order to receive the turn when it is passed. Each speaker must not only avoid breaking or altering the rhythm of the poem, but also must remember to pass the turn on to some other person in time for that person to continue the recitation without breaking the rhythm.

5. Next (or as a separate exercise), give pairs of students poems to work on in the above way. Again, students should recite the poem aloud to become familiar with it, and to find the proper rhythm. Then, they must divide the lines between themselves and practice reciting the poems without breaking the natural rhythm. Partners may agree to speak some of the lines in unison, but not all of them. Creative line distribution can enhance the performance of the poem. Finally, each team "performs" the recitation of its poem for the class.

Option: Lists of words or numbers can be used as text for the above exercise, either for the sake of convenience or in order to learn the lists (especially at lower levels). Numbers can be used, e.g., "one thirty-one, one thirty-two, one thirty-three," etc. Months can also be used, e.g., "January, February, March," etc.

The Alphabet: A Voice and Ensemble Warm-up

This exercise is a vocal production exercise focusing on control of articulation, breathing, pacing and rhythm (alternating stress). The ensemble nature of the exercises requires close listening. Using the alphabet as a text helps students learn to pronounce the names of the letters of the alphabet. Spelling words verbally is, of course, a useful communication strategy. Especially when pronunciation falls short.

Step 1: Recite the alphabet in unison, always maintaining an ensemble sound which sounds like one strong voice instead of ten loosely organized voices. Establish a strong steady "beat" throughout the recitation.

Step 2: Practice breath control by reciting the alphabet on one breath. The initial intake of air should be a deep breath taken by the group in unison. The teacher gives the command: "Ready, breath!" Then the recitation begins. Breathing should be paced so that one complete breath is expelled during recitation, and no additional inhalation is required. Repeat this exercise several times, slowing down the pace of the recitation each time.

Step 3: Repeat the recitation in phrases ranging from three to ten letters, altering volume and pace, requiring students to listen closely so as to mimic you. The students as a group try to match both volume and pace throughout, while reciting in unison. Point out that a soft volume should be no less comprehensible than a louder volume; articulation should always be specific.

Step 4: Repeat the recitation five letters at a time, with the students repeating each set of five letters after you. For each set of five letters, give major and minor stress, establishing an alternating stress pattern. Vary the stress pattern, speed, and volume for each set. (See example below.) Students should be able to reproduce your pattern, and retain a clear unison. Remember: one breath per alphabet.

Example:

TEACHER: a b c̀ d e   TEACHER: p̀ q r̀ s t̀
STUDENTS: repeat   STUDENTS: repeat

TEACHER: f g̀ h i j̀   TEACHER: ù v w x̀ y
STUDENTS: repeat   STUDENTS: repeat

TEACHER: k l m ǹ o   TEACHER: z̀
STUDENTS: repeat   STUDENTS: repeat

Controlling Sounds while Producing a Text

Exercise 1

Using a text of five to ten lines, have students practice speaking (reading) the text aloud with carefully controlled articulation, stress, intonation, and vowel sounds. To practice vocal control, have them practice speaking the text very slowly (in slow motion) at first, concentrating on well-produced sounds. Make suggestions for improving vowel and consonant problems. Gradually have them speed up their delivery. They should attempt to maintain vocal control and the "feelings" of the various sounds.

Next, have them read the text aloud. Impose the following variations on them as they read: read slower, read faster, emphasize vowels more, emphasize consonants more (exaggerate if necessary), use a lower voice, use a higher voice, speak in a whisper (but clearly).

Have everyone practice some or all of these variations alone or in pairs using dialogue. Also have the class observe as you coach individuals through this exercise. Instruct the individual readers by suggesting strategies for improving vocal production. The observing students should observe how well the instructions are followed, and the effect the variations have on vocal production. Students should also notice the effects of individual vocal habits on vocal flexibility.

Exercise 2

Use the slow-to-fast techniques with stress practice. Students can read texts that have the stressed syllables marked. They should speed up as they succeed in controlling the alternating stress pattern at the slower speed.

Exercise 3

Use the slow-to-fast technique to practice controlling the placement of resonation. Students read a long sentence, slowly, feeling the resonation. In this exercise, it is not possible to read too slowly. The resonation should be felt and "savored" as if it was being eaten. The speed of the readings should then be increased gradually, and the reader should attempt to maintain the feeling of the resonation.

THE BODY

Words alone cannot fulfill all of our communication needs. We must use our bodies to communicate. We must also pick up signals from watching other people. Instruct students to notice that when words are eliminated from communication, the animation of the body can compensate. This fact is observable as people become more animated and gesticulate with greater frequency when a point they are trying to communicate is continually misunderstood. This is also observable in the exercise below.

Exercise

1. Have students think of a short story, such as an anecdote, folk tale, or fable. Choose a volunteer to tell the story out of sight of the

audience, e.g., behind a screen, hidden around a corner, or standing behind the group. The student then tells the same story in full view of the audience. Encourage the teller to illustrate the story using hands, and movement. The audience should be observing the performer carefully. After the speaker is finished, ask the audience to comment on the physical expression of the story. How did the teller use eyes, face, hands, and body to tell the story? Repeat with other volunteers. Ask story tellers to comment on their own performance. Is it easier, or more difficult, to tell a story using the body? Is it more difficult to use the body when "performing"? With each experience the students should become more perceptive observers.

2. Ask another volunteer to tell a story without words, illustrating as much as possible with the body, "charades" style. It does not matter if the group does not fully comprehend the story. The teller should simply concentrate on the story and try to illustrate as much of it as possible. When the story is finished, the class can say what they think the story was about. Then, the teller retells the story using words and gestures.

3. Finally, have a student tell a story using absolutely no body movement except in the face and breathing apparatus. The teller should stand facing the audience with arms hanging loosely and with shoulders relaxed. Eye contact should be maintained with the group at all times. Eye contact is, of course, a visual aid to communication. What the teller lacks in the way of movement opportunities he or she should make up for in vocal expression. Encourage the teller to try to make effective use of stress, intonation, pacing, and volume. Let other students try this. Discuss the feeling of being without gesture. Discuss the feeling of being without gesture while facing an audience. How does that feeling compare with the feeling that something you are doing is being misread, or the feeling that everyone around you uses gestures that are not part of your physical vocabulary? How do we use movement to increase our confidence? How do gestures increase our ability to express ourselves? How can we relax physically in strange situations and how will physical relaxation help us communicate? (*Answer*: Your instrument (your body) is more flexible when it is relaxed. Posture and relaxed, controlled breathing facilitate voice control. A controlled voice helps us speak clearly and confidently.)

The Body and the Voice

What happens when we become nervous? Our bodies become tense, our voices sometimes become less controlled, and then our nervousness increases because we realize that we look and sound as nervous as we feel. Notice how students speaking before a group will avoid eye contact with others, especially in moments of nervousness. This is a natural reaction to being nervous. It is a coping strategy we use to avoid revealing, through eye contact, that we are nervous or unsure. In addition, it may be appropriate and respectful in some cultures to avoid eye contact with those to whom one is speaking. The trouble is that eye contact is important for communication in the English-speaking world. When situations become uncomfortable (as they often can for second-language speakers), we need to maintain eye contact more than ever.

A flexible and controlled voice is also an asset in uncomfortable situations. What causes our voices to become thin or shaky when we are nervous? Why do we sometimes find ourselves gasping for air when we try to speak? One frequent cause is that our breathing becomes erratic and out of control. To avoid this problem on stage, actors learn about breathing and how it influences vocal production.

Exercise

Build the exercise on story telling without movement (see part 3 above) into an exercise that focuses on relaxation, eye contact and breathing. Be sure students are facing the audience, maintaining eye contact constantly, moving the eyes from one person to another, avoiding no one. They should also stand relaxed, limply, and more or less motionless except for breathing and eye movement. The weight should be evenly distributed over both feet. Shoulders and face muscles should be relaxed.

To teach the standing position, have the class stand up and stretch a bit, shaking hands, feet, arms, and legs, rolling heads and loosening the face through movement. Then have everyone take the position described above. Move from student to student identifying areas of tension. Instruct students to let their arms hang loose, drop their shoulders, breathe deeply and easily filling the air space, and avoid shifting from foot to foot. Instruct students to concentrate on each area of the body, individually, and identify and attempt to eliminate tension. Give them time to relax themselves. Instruct them to feel the breathing apparatus at work and to memorize the feeling of relaxed controlled breathing. Point out that they will want to recall that feeling in less relaxed situations. Self-relaxation takes practice so you will want to repeat this relaxation process in future sessions. This is a good way to begin a play rehearsal.

Next, have students sit in chairs arranged in a semicircle. They should sit with both feet on the floor and attempt to maintain relaxation. Each student takes a turn standing in the limp, relaxed, nearly motionless position facing the group. Eye contact should be maintained. Tension is sought out and eliminated. Tell students to do a mental inventory of the body in search of tension. Talk them through this if necessary, e.g., "Your shoulders are raised up again, drop them!" "You are biting your lip." "Maintain eye contact," etc. Watch for areas of tension. Shoulder shrugging, shifting from foot to foot, averting the eyes, and other extraneous movements are natural defense mechanisms. Identify them as such when students use them, and tell them to try to relax without them.

This exercise is not easy. Students will want to fidget and avert their eyes. They will not feel able to relax at first. This is partly because we use movement to make ourselves feel comfortable. For every situation we are in, our bodies, consciously or not, find a "stance." With posturing and movement we fortify ourselves. This exercise helps students become more aware of how they express themselves physically. It also gives them practice controlling their habits.

Once the above points have been made, give students a vocal task to carry out so they can practice vocal control, maintaining relaxation, eye contact, and physical control while their bodies are stripped of their most common posturing defenses. Have them tell a story or recite a poem. Ask them questions or let the class interview them. Tell them to work to learn to take advantage of relaxation and breathing to control the voice. Encourage experimentation with vocal variety, e.g., "Use the higher and lower parts of your range. Use stress to enhance your story. Slow down and be specific so we can hear the difference between your th and your d." Be sure that they are maintaining eye contact with someone in the audience at all times, and help them, through coaching, to remain in the "neutral" position. Your constant coaching will help the observing students to focus their attention on each performer's physical tensions and efforts to overcome them.

Finally, instruct students to memorize the feeling of relaxing and breathing properly in the tense situation created by this exercise. Tell them to practice relaxing in real life situations. Relaxation is a valuable coping strategy in difficult situations that make us nervous. Through practice, relaxation can become an automatic reaction to a feeling of nervousness. For the well-trained language speaker, it is a valuable coping strategy to have in one's repertoire.

Acting without Words

When trying to communicate to an audience through movement, an actor must move specifically, avoiding extraneous actions that distract the audience from the movements they should see. The three exercises below should be approached as problems that can be solved through experimentation.

Have individuals perform these exercises for the class. Each "actor" repeats one exercise several times. Between performances, the teacher and classmates make suggestions and ask questions that "direct" the performer toward a more realistic and communicative performance.

Exercise 1:

DROP THE BOX A person standing at a bus stop drops his/her parcel, and the contents scatter. The person picks up the possessions and puts them back in the parcel. To make the pantomime appear real, the actor must imagine actual items as they are looked at and handled. Through natural actions, the actor should try to "show" the audience what the items are.

Exercise 2:

OPEN THE BOX A person enters a room with a parcel, opens the parcel, and uses the object inside. The actor should clearly demonstrate to the audience what the object is, without resorting to unrealistic behavior. Be specific and economical in movement.

Exercise 3:

WHERE AM I? An actor chooses an imaginary location and character, then performs a simple pantomime that clearly shows where the character is.

Physical Ensemble Warm-ups

I include the following three exercises as pre-rehearsal warm-ups. They are easy, fun, physical games that warm-up your actors and bring them together into a lively ensemble.

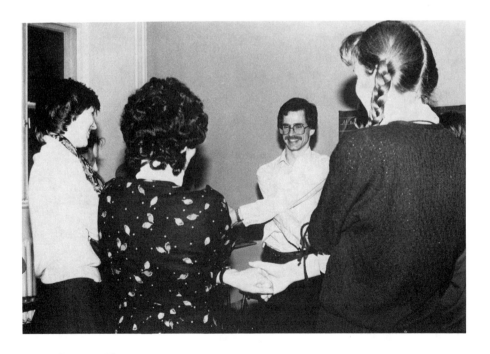

Squeeze Play

Exercise: Squeeze Play

Students and teacher stand in a circle, cross arms in front, and clasp the fore-arms or hands of the people standing on each side. Then, a one-handed squeeze signal is given by the director to one of the people at his/her side. That person, upon feeling the teacher's signal, passes the squeeze on to the next person. When the squeeze returns to the teacher, the tempo is picked up, increased, or decreased by the teacher. (The space between each squeeze sets the tempo. Since each person controls one squeeze, immediately after feeling a squeeze, then each person can vary the tempo. The group communicates by being sensitive to the tempos set by the teacher. The teacher should be able to tell if tempos are being maintained by the length of time it takes for the squeezes to travel full circle. The teacher can also vary the number of squeezes.

Exercise: Trust I—Pass the Body

One actor stands as stiffly as possible in a circle created by fellow actors. With feet planted in the center, the stiff actor falls against the circle and is passed and pushed around the circle by the others. The actor must remain stiff in order to enjoy the ride.

Pass the Body

Exercise: Trust II—Catch

Actors work in teams. Each actor falls backward into the arms of a partner.

PRACTICING COMMUNICATION STRATEGIES

The challenge faced by language teachers is to help learners bridge the gap between passive knowledge of a language and active communication with it. Communicating in a second language requires the learner to learn to play roles, understand the roles played by others, listen and react to what one sees and hears, compensate for missing skills or information, form messages from limited linguistic resources, and improvise. Second-language users must think on their feet.

The following exercises are designed to give learners experience interacting in the second language. Only through experience will a learner develop strategies for active communication.

Creating a Simple Role-playing Situation

You can easily create your own instructions for role playing situations in order to give students the opportunity to "use" the language on which you are focusing. Keep instructions simple. Describe straightforward situations including: who the characters are, where they are, and what they are to do. It is a common technique to include "conflict" to give actors a reason for interacting. I often give actors different sets of instructions so that each actor knows what his or her character "wants," but not necessarily what the other characters want. It is, then, the actor's task to discover and adapt to the motivations of the other characters. You might give the actors a list of useful language to prepare them for role playing. The following format is common:

Asking permission:

Would it be possible _____

Could I _____

Couldn't I _____

How about _____

Would it be alright if I _____

Can I _____

May I _____

Would it be inconvenient for me to _____

What if I were to _____

Do you think I could _____

Making excuses:

I'm very sorry, but we must _____

I'm afraid you can't. We have to _____

Sorry, but _____

You've picked a bad time because _____

The problem is _____

That wouldn't work because _____

No, because _____

Absolutely not. You see _____

The following example of simple role playing instructions could accompany the language examples listed above.

ROLE ONE: You work in an office. You are a _____ in a _____. (Fill in the type of company and job with something relevant to your students' interests.) Ask your boss for a vacation. You would like to take it next month. The boss should say "yes," you feel, because you have not had a vacation in over a year. Your contract includes two weeks per year of vacation. Don't accept "no" for an answer.

ROLE TWO: You work in an office. You are a _____ in a _____. (Same as above.) Your employee will ask you for a vacation. This is one of your best employees and you feel he/she deserves a vacation, but you must say "no." You have large projects that must be finished in three months. You need him/her to do research for you. He/she is the only person who is familiar enough with certain aspects of the project. No one else can help you.

VARIATION OF ROLE ONE: Ask your boss for a vacation, but don't pressure him/her. You realize your boss needs your help on these important projects. You haven't had a vacation in over a year, though, so if there is any way you can get one, do so. If not, find out when you can take your vacation.

Scripted Dialogues

When creating scripts through improvisation, actors sometimes carry pieces of paper on which their own lines are written and not those of the others in the scene. As they rehearse, actors continue to write and edit their own personal scripts. The only way to know how one's scene partners are developing their own lines is to listen.

I remember playing a minor role in the musical *Gypsy*. The publisher provided scripts for the speaking roles in which only one character's *cues* and *lines* were written. In order to "learn" the scenes we were in, we had to listen and react accordingly to what the other actors said and did. We couldn't "read" the entire scenes, and were, thus, prevented from burying our faces and voices in our books. The result was a more spontaneous, realistic performance.

Instead of giving your students dialogues to read, give them only the lines they have to speak, and if necessary, their cues.

Example:

Role 1   Student 1: Excuse me. How do I get to the lake from here?

Cue: . . . . . or driving?

Student 1: I'm walking.

Cue: . . . . . you'll see it.

Student 1: Is that where they rent boats?

Cue: . . . . . I'm not from here.

Student 1: Ok. Thanks a lot.

Role 2   Cue: . . . . . to the lake from here?

Student 2: It's easy. Are you walking or driving?

Cue: . . . . . walking.

Student 2: Then, go down this hill, and turn right, and you'll see it.

Cue: . . . . . rent the boats?

Student 2: I don't know. You'll have to ask someone else. I'm not from here.

Cue: . . . . . Thanks a lot.

Student 2: You're welcome.

Scenes with Few Words

The following exercise often yields surprising and quite creative results. Give the written instructions below to the students. The students can interpret them as they wish. Groups of two to four are appropriate. Repeat three times.

Exercise

Instructions for students: Create a short scene based on one of the following ideas. You may use only six words or three sentences. *Remember*: Actions speak louder than words.

the beginning	finding	reuniting	protesting
the end	refusing	teaching	preventing
leaving	permitting	growing old	enjoying
arriving	death	dominating	
searching	birth	submitting	

Making Conversation

Exercise

Each student writes one sentence on a piece of paper. Collect the papers and redistribute them to the class so that no student gets his or her own paper. Divide the class into groups of three or four students. Allow five to ten minutes for groups to meet and discuss or practice a scene. The scene can be about anything, but it must include the sentences written on the pieces of paper. Class assembles. Each group improvises its scene. Scenes should be smoothly flowing conversations. Repeat the exercise several times, eliminating the practice session as an option. Each team can write sentences for the other team to perform. The content of the sentences should have no restrictions and can be seen as a challenge from one team to another.

The sentences written on the pieces of paper should be worked into each scene so that they seem to belong. The students must work creatively to find ways to incorporate three or more seemingly unrelated sentences into one coherent conversation. Each participant should respond to the conversations and actions of the others. That is, a scene should not be three or four separate conversations, but an integrated, sincere interaction. Students should try to develop the scenes so that they actually "go somewhere." Encourage them to add anything they wish in terms of dialogue and action to develop themes. Remember that the object is not to be entertaining as much as it is to create realistic interactions. Between rounds, you should discuss ways to make these conversations seem more realistic. Observe especially how well the "actors" listen and respond to their partners. Emphasize the various strategies the actors employ to make transitions from one topic to another.

Series Role Playing

Exercise

Create a series of short, related scenes (see example below). Choose volunteers to play Scene 1. Give them short verbal instructions. They can fill in their own details, and develop the scene in any direction they choose. While the scene is being enacted, the rest of the class watches. When the scene has been played for a reasonable amount of time, end it. Don't cut them off if they are in the middle of a good exchange that seems to be going somewhere. Don't feel, either, like you have to stop them if they seem to stumble a bit, or if silence reigns. Find a happy medium. The only time you really should intervene in the middle of the scene is if the students are not concentrating on the task.

After Scene 1, choose different students to play the same roles and any new roles that have been added in Scene 2. The actors then play Scene 2, using all the information they gained from observing Scene 1. Any new decisions are left to the actors. Repeat the process until all scenes have been played.

If students begin this exercise with some hesitation, they will relax once they have started. They do not need to pre-plan what they are going to say. The "script" should be developed as they improvise. Don't let them ask you what to do during the scene. You are not part of the scene. Instruct them to ignore the audience; entertainment is not the object. They should simply try to make the language real and to let the conversation develop naturally.

Actors must be alert for cues and information given by the other actors in the scene. If, for example, one actor states, "we have been married 20 years," then the other actor must respond appropriately, i.e., behave as if the couple has been married 20 years. The series of scenes should be interrelated so that all information given in previous scenes is applicable to subsequent scenes. Since the actors change but the characters remain the same, the audience members must watch each scene closely so that they can step into the shoes of the characters.

Just before a scene is played, I usually give the actors a few minutes to discuss any details they want to with their partners. During this time, when the actors are out of the room, I might instruct the audience to watch for certain behavior. For example, in Scene 5 the audience watches to see how the seating in the restaurant will be handled, i.e., when six people approach a table in a restaurant, how do they negotiate (non-verbally or verbally) their seating arrangement? The actors don't know that we are watching for that particular action.

Sample Scenario for Series Role Playing

Scene 1: Couple number one, at home, discusses conflicting ideas about where to go on their upcoming vacation. Finally, they agree.

Scene 2: Couple number two arrives that same evening. Couple number one tells them of the travel plans and invites them to come along.

Scene 3: Both couples arrive together at a vacation cottage/room/hotel or other dwelling. They move in and explore. They begin to plan the next day and the coming week.

Scene 4: A local couple, couple number three, who are friends of couple number one, arrives at the location used for scene three, as planned, for an evening's visit. They meet couple number two for the first time.

Scene 5: Next evening at a restaurant, all three couples arrive and are seated by a waiter. They order and talk.

After the series is over, use the experience to discuss language and communication points. Language "needs" that the students have should emerge in the course of the acting. You, the teacher, should take notes as you watch. I sometimes use a tape recorder in order to play back sections of the improvisation. In addition to discussing vocabulary and grammar problems, we also discuss the unspoken assumptions that are manifested in the acting. Actions are examined. For example, when new visitors enter the house (Scenes 2 and 4), the people already in the room usually stand to greet them. Our discussions inevitably include matters of custom, courtesy, and variations in ritual. We also discuss how well the actors listened to and "played off of" each other. In doing so, we relate role-playing strategies to real life: We do not always know what others will say and do, but we communicate most effectively when we quickly recognize and adapt to what others say and do.

Audience-Directed Role Playing

Exercise

Two or more actors are chosen from the class. They quickly decide for themselves who they are going to be, e.g., two friends, professional colleagues, customer and salesperson, landlord and tenant, etc. They tell the class who they are and then begin a conversation that clearly illustrates their relationship, while avoiding cliches. When the relationship has been established for the audience to see, the teacher or a student commands, "Stop!" The actors stop and one audience member commands the actors to perform a given function, such as, "Ask!" The actors pause only momentarily in order to receive the command and then must continue the scene, integrating the command. When the function has been clearly illustrated, another command is given in the same way, and so on. Each time a command is given the actors should maintain concentration on their acting so as not to "break character."

Below is a list of functions that could be used for this exercise. The actors must consider the reciprocal nature of role playing as they "play off of" (i.e., interact with) each other. For many of the functions the actors will have to play opposing roles, that is, one actor will advise (if the command is "Advise!") and the other will receive the advice and react to it. Remind the actors that it is not necessary to *entertain* the audience. They simply need to make the interaction as real as possible. The audience may allow the acting to continue for periods of time without interjecting a new command. The audience would do this, for example, if they wish to see how the scene will develop. The actors are obliged to maintain their roles and continue acting regardless of the frequency of commands.

advise	compliment	patronize	request	interrogate
guess	promise	scold	apologize	
instruct	lie	reject	ask	
complain	hint	praise	tell	
criticize	accuse	concede	congratulate	

Moods in Situations

Exercise

Begin this exercise as you would begin a simple role playing activity. For example, if you wanted to let your students practice the language used when ordering in a restaurant, you might choose two customers and a waiter and let the students improvise the situation. In the course of the role playing, you can take notes of comments you want to make later regarding appropriate language needs. You might want to suggest language to fulfill various functions that the players need to execute. You could list alternatives on the board. For example, making suggestions to your dining partner:

How about ——————————————————————————?
Would you like ————————————————————————?
Do you want to try ———————————————————————?
Have you ever had ———————————————————————?
I recommend ——————————————————————————?
Why not try some ————————————————————————?

Once the situation and language have been established through improvisation and coaching by the teacher, add some characteristics to the players' "characters" as follows. Class members write adjectives on pieces of paper. Make enough of these pieces so that each actor has three. Have the actors start role playing the situation again. You, as the director, call out "one," cueing each actor to take on characteristics that correspond with one of the adjectives he or she has been given. At this point, each audience member writes down, for each actor, the adjective that he or she thinks the actor is playing. When they have had time to do this, you call out, "two," and the actors alter their characters to play different adjectives. Again, the audience attempts to write down the adjectives they think they are seeing. Then, command "three." Again, the actors alter their characters and the audience records their guesses. How the actors choose to "play" their characters is up to them. They should, however, try to make it clear which adjectives they are playing without actually saying the word. It is the actor's job to make sure that the role playing continues nonstop as long as it takes, until the teacher calls an end to it.

When the role playing finishes, go over the students' adjectives and compare them to the adjectives that the actors were actually playing. In addition to learning some adjectives that are used to describe people (you can provide a list of specific ones, or let the students provide their own), students practice the language of the situation you choose. (In this case it is restaurant ordering, but don't feel compelled to restrict yourself to everyday situations. Choose situations that are relevant to the needs of your class.) Students also experience being misinterpreted. Even when they think they have been quite clear, students will sometimes discover that they have been misunderstood.

For example, the actors might have played the following adjectives: curious, tired, hungry. But a classmate might write: Actor's name: pushy, bored, sick.

Devil's Advocate

Exercise

Students think of a topic, idea, or point of view they would like to defend. Give them time to organize their thoughts and take a few notes. One student then begins by expressing an opinion including any supporting arguments. Then, choose one volunteer, or appoint a student, to play the role of devil's advocate. The devil's advocate must argue against the opinion of the other student. The devil's advocate need not disagree with the other student in reality, but he or she should nevertheless make as strong a case as possible in opposition to the other student. The object is, of course, to have students play opposing roles for the sake of evaluating two or more sides of an issue and for practicing effective arguing skills. Set a time limit for each pair. Between topics, pause to discuss and evaluate the debating strategies used. Who argues most effectively? Why? List useful language on the board for the benefit of those waiting to debate.

Variation: Same as above except after each team has debated for a reasonable amount of time, the two students trade roles and resume debate on the same topic.

Ensemble Poetry

Choose a group of poems, perhaps around a common theme, or one long poem for the students to use.

Exercise

The class is divided into groups of three to five students. Each group is assigned one poem or one section of a poem. Each group rehearses its text for 20 minutes (or longer), finding ways to interpret it vocally and physically. Inform students that there is a time limit so that they will work quickly and efficiently, in ensemble, to interpret the poem and coordinate the performance of it. Division of lines and mixture of solo and choral voices is left to the discretion of the group. Remind students to use articulation, intonation, phrasing, and pacing to interpret the poem. Anything goes. It is not necessary for the poems to be memorized. Because rehearsal time is so restricted, students must work fast. The performances, although somewhat rough, are usually quite entertaining.

Variation: As an option, use a story instead of a poem. Narratives are especially appropriate.

Silence

What are the various meanings that silence can have in interaction? Different cultures react differently to silence. When questioned, is it always necessary to respond immediately? (Not in all cultures.) What does silence imply when it is in response to a statement of opinion? The following exercises explore silence.

Exercise 1

A pause, used as a dramatic device, is sometimes referred to as a "Pinter pause" because Harold Pinter exploits pauses so effectively in his plays and sketches. Have two groups work separately on the following section of a play by Pinter. One group should omit the pauses, and the other group should use the pauses for maximum effect. The pieces can be memorized as an option, but a dramatic reading should suffice to make the point. (Other Pinter sketches suggested for this exercise are "The Black and White," and "Request Stop." Both sketches can be found in Harold Pinter's *Complete Works: Two*, Grove Press, Inc., N.Y.)

The scene below is the opening scene of Harold Pinter's one-act play, "A Slight Ache." A man and woman are seated at their breakfast table. The man is reading a newspaper.

Flora: Have you noticed the honeysuckle this morning?

Edward: The what?

Flora: The honeysuckle.

Edward: Honeysuckle? Where?

Flora: By the back gate, Edward.

Edward: Is that honeysuckle? (*He lowers his paper*) I thought it was—convolvulus, or something.

Flora: But you know it's honeysuckle.

Edward: I tell you I thought it was convolvulus.

(*There is a pause*)

Flora: It's in wonderful flower.

Edward: I must look.

Flora: The whole garden's in flower this morning. The clematis. The convolvulus. Everything. I was out at seven. I stood by the pool.

Edward: Did you say—that the convolvulus was in flower?

Flora: Yes.

Edward: But good God, you just denied there was any.

Flora: I was talking about the honeysuckle.

Edward: About the what?

Flora: (*calmly*) Edward—you know that shrub outside the toolshed—

Edward: Yes, yes.

Flora: —that's convolvulus.

Edward: That?

Flora: Yes.

Edward: Oh.

> (*There is a pause*)

Edward: I thought it was japonica.

Flora: Oh, good Lord, no.

Edward: Pass the teapot, please.

> (*There is a pause.* Flora *pours a cup of tea for Edward and adds milk*)
>
> I don't see why I should be expected to distinguish between these plants. It's not my job.

Flora: You know perfectly well what grows in your garden.

Edward: Quite the contrary. It is clear that I don't.

> (*There is a pause.* Flora *looks at Edward, rises and moves up* LC *on to the rostrum*)

Flora: I was up at seven. I stood by the pool. The peace. And everything in flower. The sun was up. You should work in the garden this morning. We could put up the canopy.

Edward: The canopy? What for?

Flora: To shade you from the sun.

Edward: Is there a breeze?

Flora: A slight one.

Edward: It's very treacherous weather, you know.

> (*There is a pause.* Flora *faces up stage*)

Flora: Do you know what today is?

Edward: (*consulting the date on the top of his paper*) Saturday.

Flora: It's the longest day of the year.

Exercise 2

In groups of two to four, create short sketches in which the only required element is at least one *meaningful* pause. The words and actions should serve to "set up" the pause so that it has maximum impact.

Contrasting Character Types

Exercise

Have two or more groups of students create and perform short scenes based on a scenario. Although the groups use the same scenario, the characters they are to play are different. The performances should reflect the difference in characters.

Scenario: Character one asks character two to do something and explains why it needs to be done. Character two understands why this action should be taken, but will not do it and explains why. Character one reacts to what character two has said.

Set one: Character one is an authority figure (president of a company, mayor, boss, police officer, etc.), character two is an employee or subordinate of character one.

Set two: Character one is a panhandler. Character two is a passerby.

Text Manipulation

Exercise

Students rehearse a dialogue in pairs (trios, quartets, etc.) and then perform for the group. The dialogues do not need to be memorized. Each pair of students has the same dialogue, but must interpret the dialogue using a different one of the following variables to show the relationship between characters: love, hate, suspicion, flirtation, superiority/inferiority, disgust, fear, indifference, admiration, respect, humility, brashness, thankfulness, joy, ecstasy, hilarity. This exercise is fun. Students should be encouraged to use either a realistic or an exaggerated acting style. Each performance should be a stark contrast to all the other performances. After the first round of performances, have each pair perform again and instruct them to carry their interpretation further, making the contrast between scenes even greater.

Any simple dialogue will do. The words are less important than the acting. Below is an example.

DIALOGUE:

A: So, you're all finished here, aren't you?

B: Yes. Finished.

A: Are you leaving then?

B: My bags are packed.

A: Aren't you going to say goodbye to the others?

B: To whom?

A: You know . . . everyone.

B: Why?

A: Why not?

B: Well . . . , hm . . . , I don't know. I think I'll just say goodbye to you.

A: All right.

B: Goodbye.

A: Goodbye.

Option: Instead of using a dialogue for the above exercise, use a scenario. For example: B appears to be going away. B's bags are packed. A asks B if B is really leaving and whether or not B is going to say goodbye to anyone. B replies.

Cold Reading

This exercise is for oral production work. At auditions, actors are sometimes handed scripts they have never seen before. They are given a short amount of time to look at a specific scene and then they are asked to "read," i.e., perform, the scene before the casting director. This reading is not expected to be a polished, complete performance of the script, yet the actor's reading must reflect an appropriate interpretation of the script and show off some of the actor's talents.

This actually is not a reading exercise as much as it is a vocal production exercise. Having students read aloud in class has questionable value in terms of teaching reading skills but "cold reading" practice guides students toward a practical use of their ability to read aloud. A brief review of the script before reading aloud gives students only a superficial understanding of a text, yet the students are ready to benefit from reading the text aloud. Free from the need to think of words or structures, students instead can concentrate on exploring and manipulating *sound* and its potential for communication.

Exercise

Step 1: Pass out short "easy" selections of prose, poetry, or scenes from plays—one reading per student. If you have scenes including two or more characters, then students can perform together, but they need not practice together during Step 2.

Step 2: Give students time (5 to 10 minutes, but adjust time at your discretion) to review selections. During this time they should be encouraged to read aloud if they wish.

Step 3: Have each student read a selection aloud for the class two or more times as if at an audition. This reading should be an interpretive reading insofar as possible, although they will probably be quite rough at this point. Suggestions should be made by the teacher and audience members (fellow students) for improving the readings. Students should attempt to incorporate suggestions with each successive reading. All students should try to incorporate suggestions made to classmates into their own readings as well. As with many exercises, students should be aware that they should try to develop their ability to "take direction," i.e., benefit from the criticisms and suggestions of the audience.

Quick Speeches

Students whose fields of study or professions require them to give presentations in a foreign language can benefit from practicing in class. When given several days to prepare a presentation on a subject of their choice, and with a time range of say 5 to 20 minutes, students' speeches do not always turn out to be as eloquent as all the preparation time and flexibility might suggest. Speeches are often too long and disorganized or rambling. Several days might be required to give everyone a chance to speak.

In order to give students experience covering a subject in a reasonably short period of time, I put them through "quick speeches."

Exercise

Speeches are announced at the beginning of class. Students have 5 to 10 minutes to choose a topic from a list and make notes for a presentation, which is limited to five minutes. The time limit is stressed. At least seven students should get to speak in one class period and sometimes more. If speeches last over five minutes, give them a signal to "conclude." Take notes as the speeches are being given. After each speech make suggestions for improving content and delivery.

This situation best reflects the conditions of a job interview, admissions interview, having to summarize a situation in a business meeting, or other situations in which the students will find they have a very short time to organize and present significant thoughts.

Below is a sample list of speech topics. (You, of course, should construct a list which is appropriate for your particular group of students):

my education

native art in my country

aspect X of my profession (choose one)

summary of a local, national, or world current event (choose one)

the English language in my country (or any second language in a non-native speaking country)

night life in this city

the structure of my government/the American government/a Swiss bank/ a multinational oil company/trade unions in my country

the Japanese tea ceremony

the Polish community in Chicago, Puerto Rican community in New York, the Vietnamese community in San Francisco, the American Community in Kuwait, etc.

agriculture in my country

the geography of my country

Editing Speeches

In order to learn to write well, students must learn to edit. In order to learn to write and perform good speeches, students must learn to edit their speeches. The editing of a speech should include the editing of the perform- ance of the speech as well as the text. Editing should be based on rehearsals or trial runs of the speech.

Exercise

Assign speeches and give students time to write and practice them. Set a reasonable time limit for the length of the speeches. Instead of having one presentation only, have students present their speeches at least twice for the class. The first presentation should be given for the purpose of receiving constructive criticism. The class members should offer criticisms and sugges- tions for each speech. The teacher should guide these sessions to make sure that they are constructive. Students are then given time to rework and rehearse their speeches. A final presentation is given, and again, students receive criticism. This second criticism session should include observations on how and how well presenters incorporate the suggestions given after the first presentation.

Each student will, of course, spend more time observing speakers than actually speaking in this exercise. One object of this exercise is to give students the opportunity to observe classmates attempting to solve the problems which stand in the way of good speech making. Make the problems of each individual speaker the problems of the class by asking all students to help find solutions to these problems.

Charades

Charades is a natural game for the language classroom. It is an excellent way for students and teachers to relax together, get to know each other, use language (both verbal and non-verbal), and have a good time. It is ideal for interclass competitions since two teams are required. A large number can play but everyone does not have to "act" for the game to work. Many communication skills are used in a game of charades: listening, watching, fast thinking, remembering, and negotiating, to name a few. There is a strong emphasis on non-verbal language. Students are often quite effective in using their grammatical knowledge in playing charades.

Exercise

If you know how to play charades already, then use any system that you know will work. For the basic game you need two teams, a watch with a second hand, and a pool of sentences written out on pieces of paper. If you, the teacher, write the sentences yourself, you can control the language and make sure the game is fair. Another method is to have each team write sentences for the other team to act out and guess.

A member of team 1 chooses a piece of paper at random, reads the sentence (silently), then attempts through actions alone, i.e., without words, to get teammates to say the sentence aloud, one word at a time if necessary. The actor can do nearly anything except talk and write. It is the duty of the team members who are not acting to be vocal and try to guess what the actor is trying to express. The actor can guide the team with signals (listed below).

To make the game easier, draw a blank on the board for every word in the sentence. The actor can then point to the blank he or she wishes teammates to fill. When the team guesses a word, the teacher writes the word in its blank.

There is usually a three minute time limit for each sentence. Score can be kept either by counting the number of sentences each team is able to complete or by keeping a tally of the total time taken by each team, with three minutes being the maximum possible time recorded for any single sentence.

Below are just a few of the most common signals used in charades. Your students will create their own as the game progresses.

1. If you want to indicate that the word you want to elicit is a "small word" (article, preposition, pronoun, etc.) hold your thumb and forefinger straight out, an inch apart, and curl the rest of your fingers as if to say "It's only this big." Your teammates should then begin saying small words until the correct one is uttered, at which point you react by nodding and pointing at the person who says it.

2. To signal "past tense," point back over your shoulder with your thumb. Use this when teammates have the correct word, but need to change it to past tense.

3. Hold any quantity of fingers against your inside forearm to indicate how many syllables there are in the word you are trying to elicit.

4. Move your hands as if pulling taffy to indicate that you want your teammates to keep guessing and that they are on the right track, or to indicate that they should "extend the concept" they are referring to.

5. Tugging downward on your earlobe means, "It sounds like . . . ." Follow this motion with a clear signal that will set off sound associations. For example, if you tug downward on your ear and point to your head, your teammates should respond by saying, "Sounds like

head." You nod yes. Then your teammates begin to say words that sound like head, i.e., lead, red, dead, bed, and so forth. When they say the word you are hoping for, then you point immediately to the person who said it and nod.

Feedback

This simple exercise teaches students a basic lesson in empathic communication. Students learn to play the role of "good listener" by giving feedback to be sure that the facts of a story are clear. This exercise also tightens the class ensemble as participants learn about each other through one-to-one conversation.

Exercise

Step 1: Half of the class think of stories to tell. For example, I sometimes have students think of an aspect of their cultures that foreigners do not usually know about. Instead of an anecdotal story, the information could be instructions, a description of a process, a summary of a business situation, and so forth. The story tellers should take some notes in order to organize their thoughts before telling their stories.

Step 2: The students with the stories relate them to partners chosen from the other half of the class. Each partner is instructed to give the teller feedback as the story progresses by occasionally retelling the details of the story in his own words. The original story teller thereby has the opportunity to say, "Yes, that's correct," or, "No, you misunderstood me," or, "Well, that's about 8 percent correct, but you seem to have missed an important point which is . . . ," etc. Helpful sentences like these can be listed on the blackboard before the telling begins.

Step 3: When the stories have been told, fed back, and corrected, the listeners then tell the stories that they have heard to the class as a whole. The class members give feedback as they listen. When the class has heard and understood a story, the original teller reports on the accuracy of the partner's rendition of the story.

The lessons learned in this exercise can be recalled throughout your second-language course to help students learn when, as listeners, their roles involve more than just head nodding. In many situations, the second-language speaker expects reassurance from a listener that information has been understood. Students in their roles as speakers and listeners should become sensitive to situations in which they are expected to give feedback. They also should allow listeners to give feedback in appropriate situations. Misunderstandings can result when people nod their heads in order to be "polite," rather than inform a speaker that he or she has not been understood.

Discussion Questions

In what English language situations is feedback often expected and helpful? For each of these situations, what are some specific sentences that could be used to give feedback? In the case of instructions, for example, one might say, "I understand that we must always turn off all electrical switches before dismantling the machine, but I don't understand exactly the order in which we should turn the switches off." Phone calls made for the purpose of arranging meetings often end with, "O.K. then, I'll see you next Tuesday at five o'clock." In friendly conversation, feedback is used by listeners to show a polite interest in the anecdotes of a speaker, e.g., "Oh really? You're working on a new building now?"

Improvisations

In teams, improvise one of the following situations. Be sure to demonstrate the use of feedback. Prepare for 5 to 10 minutes, then perform.

    a. inviting someone to a dinner party
    b. arranging a business meeting
    c. planning a travel itinerary
    d. giving instructions/taking orders
    e. explaining why someone cannot do something
    f. giving someone a message for someone else
    g. explaining a technical process
    h. making alternative plans, which depend on the weather

Useful Language

    Oh, I see what you're saying. You mean . . . .
    Let me see if I understand you correctly. You mean . . . .
    In other words . . . .
    Are you saying that . . . .
    Oh! Then . . . .
    So . . . .
    Let me just run through this once . . . .
    So, that means . . . .
    Let me get this straight . . . .

Job Interview

This exercise has obvious applications outside the classroom.

Exercise

Step 1: A panel of two, three, or four interviewers meets to examine a job description and to decide what type of person they are looking for to fill the job. They formulate the questions they will ask in the interview. The remainder of the class breaks into groups of three to five students per group. Each group chooses one member to be the applicant. (*Note*: at least two applicants are needed for the exercise so divide the class accordingly.) The groups examine the job description and create a fictitious background for the applicant in order to create the ideal person for the job. The group may coach the applicant on interviewing techniques.

Step 2: The panel interviews one applicant at a time. Each applicant attempts to present himself/herself as a person who fits the job description.

Step 3: The panel meets again to decide who, if anyone, they will hire.

Step 4: The panel members explain the reasons for their decision to the class (the audience and job applicants). All class members should join in the discussion and criticize the interviewing strategies used.

Sample Job Descriptions

SALES REPRESENTATIVE NEEDED: A large multinational computer firm requires a sales representative for its North American division. No previous computer experience is necessary. An expanding market requires highly motivated individuals who are good communicators. Fluency in English is a must. Other languages are desired. We provide training and a competitive salary.

EXPERIENCED BODYGUARD/DRIVER: Bodyguard/driver required for wealthy V.I.P. Must be an educated individual with excellent driving skills, professional guard experience, and impeccable references. Fluency in at least two languages including English is essential. Salary and benefits are commensurate with the position.

SIMULATIONS

A simulation is a means of activating the knowledge and language associated with topics you and your students are studying. A simulation gives participants the opportunity to practice taking on specific roles and improvising within specific situations. The assumption is that, with practice, the participants will play their roles more effectively when situations involving similar language functions occur in "real life."

Simulations are used to train people to communicate and interact in a variety of specific situations. Simulations are used, for example, to train corporate personnel in presentation and sales techniques. Cross-cultural training simulations are used to prepare business, government, and academic professionals for life in foreign cultures. Lawyers practice their craft in simulated courtroom trials; medical, civil, and government professionals simulate disaster drills; astronauts simulate activities involved in space travel; police officers simulate crime intervention techniques, and politicians simulate campaign speeches and debates.

Simulations are also effective devices for facilitating communication practice in the language classroom. Language learning takes place in the context of a culture, and "specific" situations. A simulation activity provides a specific situation within which students can practice executing language functions.

Teacher's Instructions

Simulations of varying complexity and designed for a variety of purposes are available in print, in language teaching texts, management training materials, etc. You can design your own, as well.

The following is a role playing simulation which could, as an option, be accompanied by readings and discussions dealing with its particular topic: a vocational training center in an inner-city area. The simulation is not only for those living and working in the inner-city or industry, it is also a means of practicing various communication skills including: asserting one's self, expressing opinions, convincing others, arguing effectively, finding out about the opinions of others, group problem solving, analyzing situations, and so forth. In addition, students have the opportunity to learn something about urban culture and society, e.g., vocational training, job programs in the inner city, government vs. private funding of social programs, and the various issues and attitudes related to these topics. Students well informed about these topics have the chance to teach and discuss what they know. Character study and role playing skills are also strengthened.

SIMULATION 1: THE INNER-CITY VOCATIONAL TRAINING CENTER

Note: Each step below takes time. The entire exercise including the preparation for the simulation, will require several class periods. This exercise can be used for any number of students ranging from 5 to 10. There are seven roles:

1. The chairperson
2. Ex-convict
3. Social worker
4. Small-business owner(s)
5. Industrial training consultant
6. Teacher(s)
7. Labor representative

The roles of "teacher" and "labor representative" can be eliminated. It is also possible to have two or three "teachers," and two "small business owners."

Procedure

Step 1: Lead a discussion, and if appropriate, have the class read news article(s) or other reading passages so that they understand the basic concepts and problems of the situation. Because news articles might be too difficult for some students to read, you could present the introductory content in a different way, i.e., a simplified reading passage which you construct, or a presentation and discussion in which you supply information with the help of informed students.

In cases where the students are able to read actual news reports themselves, have them work in groups of three or four. Make each group responsible for a different article. Let each group read and discuss an article until there is a general group understanding of the content. You should go from group to group, helping with explanations when asked. With your help, vocabulary is deciphered. You might want to prepare, in advance, a vocabulary list which will meet the needs of your particular group of students. It is not necessary in all cases for students to completely understand all of the vocabulary. The meanings and concepts will become clear as the simulation progresses. Next, have the class reassemble so that each group can explain its article to the class. The class discusses the general concepts of the articles.

Step 2: Next, have each student read and discuss the passage entitled "The Inner-city Vocational Training Center." Discuss the passage as a class so that all students understand the situation. Ask students to volunteer any information they have about similar situations.

Step 3: Each student is then assigned a role. Each student reads the passage that describes his/her role. Instruct students to think about their characters and create, on their own, vital facts which are missing from the character descriptions, e.g., education, specifics about their jobs, families, daily lives, etc. Meet with students individually to clarify and discuss their roles. I prefer to let my students think about their characters overnight before starting the simulation (Step 4).

Step 4: Seat the class in a circle or conference style and "simulate" the meeting. Each student plays his or her own character according to the instructions and character descriptions. The "chairperson" runs the meeting according to the instructions. You, the teacher, should stay out of the simulation. Once the simulation has begun, watch, listen, and take notes, but do not speak. Do not allow the students to appeal to you for guidance—this is their meeting. You should take notes so that you can refer to them during the post-simulation discussion (Step 5). Be sure to observe how well the students assert themselves and play their roles. Note how well each student accomplishes his/her character's goals, and how well the overall purposes of the meeting are served. Be on the lookout for language functions and vocabulary that the students could use to be more effective, but seem to lack.

Step 5: Have a post-simulation discussion. How well did the participants adhere to their roles? Were all the problems facing the training center brought out? Did people really listen to and convince each other? Was the choice of directors made wisely? What "stereotypical" preconceptions did some characters have of others? Were the preconceptions accurate? Did each character present his or her ideas clearly and convincingly? How, or why not? What problems did the students have expressing themselves? Examine solutions to these problems. Ask the students what they think the fate of the training center will be under the acting directors who were chosen in the simulation.

Reading Passage for All Participants

THE INNER-CITY VOCATIONAL TRAINING CENTER

The center is a place where adults from the inner city attend classes in order to obtain skills so that they can get jobs. All of the students are adults ranging in age from 18 to 50. All of them are poor. Most did not graduate from high school, and many have been in prison or in trouble with the law. The center holds classes to prepare students to work in local industry: automobile factories, rubber and steel plants, shipping, and for city government in construction and sanitation. The center depends on the cooperation of local industry for jobs. Some "cooperating employers" have agreed to hire students from the center to work in factories and city work crews.

Recently, there have been two serious problems that almost forced the center to close after five years. Because of government budget cuts, the center lost 90 percent of its funding. The center had been depending almost totally on money from the government's job creation program. Without government funding, there was suddenly no money for books, materials, tools, administrators' and teachers' salaries, or even rent for the center. In addition, some of the cooperating employers were threatening to stop giving jobs to the school's students because they said the students were poor workers who, "cost us more than they produce."

A group of concerned people from local industry, labor, and education were able to raise money to pay the center's costs for a two-month period, giving the center time to reorganize. More money was promised by local industry if a new group of "acting directors" could reorganize the center into a successful training school.

Today's meeting is set up to determine the problems and needs of the center, draw up a list of suggested policies for the center, and to choose a three member board of acting directors. This board must be able to solve the problems of the center and, thus, win the financial support of local industry.

This period of reorganization will be crucial. If the three new acting directors have the right attitudes, the center will be a success. If the wrong people are chosen, the center could suffer the same problems it has in the past.

Role Card 1:

The Chairperson

Your job is to run the meeting. Be sure to give everyone plenty of opportunity to express opinions, and make suggestions. The object of the meeting is to discover as much as possible about the situation, and to hear as many points of view and alternative solutions to the problems as possible. A list of suggestions must be developed and three "acting directors" must be elected by the group. The choice of three acting directors for the center will determine the survival of the center. You will be allowed to vote too, but do not prevent people with different opinions from speaking.

Procedure

1. Summarize the situation. Describe the job center and give the reasons for the meeting, in your own words.
2. Ask members to introduce themselves, telling who they are and who they represent.
3. Open the floor for a discussion of the situation, including: past problems, present needs, possible solutions, who should be on the board of directors and why, etc. Allow the discussion to proceed on its own, but make sure everyone speaks. If necessary, ask questions to get people to give more information about themselves or their ideas.
4. When the discussion has run its course, instruct the participants to cooperate in writing up a list of guidelines or suggestions for the new acting directors to follow. The main changes and policies for the center must be listed. Ask one of the members of the group to write down the suggestions. Limit the number of suggestions to 10 or less.
5. Ask for the names of anyone interested in serving on the board of acting directors for the vocational job center. Write the names of the candidates on the blackboard, if possible.
6. Have each person vote by writing three names on a piece of paper. Collect the papers, and count the votes. Announce the result.
7. End the meeting.

Role Card 2:

Ex-convict (Previous Director of Center)

Like many of the trainees at the center, you are an ex-convict and have lived in this inner-city area all of your life. You served five years in prison for an armed robbery which you committed when you were a teenager. You have been successfully rehabilitated and have won the trust and respect of the local community. You have been poor most of your life, but recently, because of opportunities offered to you by government training programs, you have begun to make a good living wage. You have become an important person in the inner-city area because of your work in the center.

You have been the director of the vocational training center for the past three months. Before you were the director, the center was poorly organized. You changed many of the policies and solved some of the most serious problems. Just when things were beginning to improve at the center, government budget cuts took away all of the money needed to run it. Now, you want to make sure the new organizers do not make the same mistakes that were made before.

Previously, there were too many government rules, which dictated how the center should be run and how the money should be spent. Money was being wasted, and teachers were not able to do a good job due to unreasonable government regulations. One problem at the center was that trainees were not taught about proper working attitudes. Bad habits were tolerated. Trainees were habitually absent or late for classes. Alcoholism is a problem and some students were drunk and disruptive in class. Some of these people were given jobs with cooperating employers, only to cause the employers to drop out of the program. You believe the center can only survive if the trainees develop proper working attitudes. Stricter enforcement of rules is needed.

You hope you will be chosen as one of the three acting directors. You must also be sure that the other two people who are chosen are people you will be able to work with and who will agree with you regarding the needs of the center. You are interested in the small business owner who is coming to the meeting. His/her influence will be necessary to obtain money and cooperation from the business community. You hope he/she is not merely interested in obtaining cheap labor for local industry. Evaluate the motives of everyone at the meeting carefully. Try to find out what types of people they are. Be suspicious and choose carefully.

Role Card 3:

Social Worker

You have been involved in social work for 10 years. You have worked in this inner-city area for the past two years. You know many of the people who will benefit from the vocational center because you have worked personally with them. Budget cuts made recently by the federal government have eliminated some of the social welfare programs that you have worked on for a long time, and this makes you angry. Among the programs you have seen eliminated are subsidized meals for school children, unemployment compensation, subsidized housing for the poor, and job training programs like the vocational training center.

This is not the first time you have seen programs go through major reorganizations because of changes in funding sources. Sometimes these changes are very good for the programs and sometimes they are very bad. If the right directors are chosen, this could be a good change. If the wrong directors are chosen, this could be the end of the center.

One of the center's problems has been the lack of machines, tools, and books for the classrooms. Because the center had to work with the government, it was almost impossible to get money for these practical things. Interestingly, it was easy to get money to give to so-called "experts" who spent the money on "researching" the center's problems and then usually made impractical suggestions.

You want to be chosen as one of the three directors of the training center. Your experience working with the people and politicians in the area will be crucial to the success of the center, you believe.

You are disturbed about the presence of certain people at this meeting. You distrust the business owner because the suburban business community has not been involved in the inner-city area in the past. The suburbs are where much of the city's wealth is spent, and whenever you have asked for financial aid in the past, the business community has grumbled that "you waste enough of our money already." Now, you fear that the business community is mainly interested in improving your area because they want to build a profitable business district there. This would only force the poor to go away to make room for the middle class "urban pioneers."

You do not trust the consultant because you think that he/she will waste too much money on researching the problems of the center, but not really be able to offer practical solutions to the problems.

You would like to see the ex-convict be chosen as a director. He/she did a good job as the previous director, and because he/she is from the same area as the students he/she understands their needs. He/she also has been rehabilitated since his/her prison days, and understands what it takes to be successful in the honest working world.

Role Card 4:

Small-Business Owner

You have many friends in the city's business community and you can assure the vocational center the financial support it will need in order to survive this difficult transitional period. You are glad the federal government has cut the social welfare budget in your city because you believe the government money was being misused and that the programs were not working. In your opinion, for example, the center was failing because students were not committed to learning marketable skills. Many students were simply coming to the center to get quick jobs. Cooperating employers complained of bad attitudes and absenteeism among the trainees they hired. You feel the situation was due to the center's poor management. You want the business community to have more control of the center for two reasons: (1) If the business community can control the way in which their money is being spent, they are likely to contribute more money to the center. Now that the government has cut funding for the center, local funding is crucial to the success of the center; (2) The business community knows best which skills the trainees need in order to survive in the working world.

Although you are from the suburbs, you want to be involved in the problems of the inner city because you believe that the problems of the city will eventually be the problems of the suburbs if they are not solved. You wish to be chosen for the board of directors so that you can do your part to help.

You want the ex-convict to be on the board of directors too. You feel that he/she would be an important member because he/she is the previous director of the job center and because he/she is a member of the local community. He/she knows what it takes to "make it" in the inner city. He/she is tough and will tolerate no nonsense from the students at the center. He/she will be needed to control discipline at the center.

You think the social worker has some good ideas because he/she has worked in the neighborhood before and knows many of the people. You wonder, though, whether he/she really is a good candidate for the board of directors. In general you feel that social workers are too idealistic and not practical enough. In some cases you feel that social workers have helped to make the system of welfare and government aid a failure because they have not been tough enough on the poor, and have tried too hard to be sympathetic and understanding. You would like to see the poor given more responsibility for their own lives. What they need is training, not money, you believe.

You do not like the training consultant because you realize he/she is only interested in winning a profitable consulting contract for his/her own business. You do not want the consultant to know you mistrust him/her. It will be easier to get rid of him/her simply by convincing the others that a consulting project is not what is needed.

Role Card 5:

Industrial Training Consultant

You are the owner of a consulting firm. Your company helps other organizations set up labor training programs. You see the vocational center as an opportunity to get a profitable contract for your own company. You can only get this if you can become one of the three acting directors and if the others on the board go along with your ideas. Do not let them know that you are mainly interested in getting this consulting contract; you know that some of the people in the meeting are more interested in the welfare of the poor people of the inner city. Do not be too eager to suggest your own company as the consulting firm. Do suggest that you think the vocational training center should try to get a grant (that is, money) from the city school board to conduct a study and reorganize the vocational training program.

Listen carefully and find out what the others want. Carefully share some of your ideas. Try to be helpful so that the group accepts you. If you decide that the others will not cooperate with you, do not agree to work as an acting director because it would waste your time. You have other projects you could spend your time on that would be more profitable. If you think that it would be easy to get the others to go along with your ideas, then try to be chosen as one of the acting directors of the center.

Role Card 6:

Teacher

You are a teacher at the center. You feel that the failure of the vocational training center in the past was due to the many rules and bureaucratic red tape that prevented the teachers and administrators from doing their jobs. The rules were often made in government offices by people who had never been to the center and did not really understand how it worked. Now, the rules can be changed since the government no longer gives money to the program.

You think that too much blame for the center's problems has been put on the students themselves. You feel that the lack of training the students received was due to the lack of a good learning atmosphere. There were not enough teachers, books, or machines. In addition, employers sometimes demanded that the center send students to work at their factories before the students were properly trained. The result was that many of the workers were not prepared for the jobs they were given.

You are not interested in being one of the acting directors yourself. You want to make sure that the new directors are going to be people who understand the problems and take realistic action to solve them. There must be more equipment and fewer rules. Industry must help out if they expect to get qualified, reliable workers from the program. Question all of the people who are hoping to become acting directors to be sure that you choose the best ones. Help the other people in this meeting understand the problems, as you see them, so that they vote for the best people as acting directors.

Role Card 7:

Labor Representative

You are the director of personnel and training for a large auto factory. Your factory will hire people from the center if the new directors will change certain aspects of the center's operation. You are at this meeting to listen to the problems and make suggestions. You hope the new acting directors will be sensible and more willing to listen to you than the last group was. You insist that a clampdown on discipline is necessary. Too many students from the center were "problem employees" the last time your company hired students from the center. They were often absent from work, and some came late or drunk. Some of them were argumentative and did not get along with the other employees. In the past, machines were damaged by reckless students. One of the problems as you see it is that, in the past, the directors at the center have been very casual about insisting that students come to class or their jobs, every day.

You should suggest that more machine skills be taught at the center. Your company might be willing to provide some shop space and machines for practical classes if the center's directors seem to be willing to solve the problems of discipline and work attitudes.

Interview the people who want to be directors and make sure you vote for the ones who will discipline the workers. Remind everyone at the meeting that your company is only interested in giving jobs to students from the center if the arrangement is profitable.

If you think that the other two directors chosen will be people who will agree with your point of view, then volunteer to serve as one of the acting directors.

SIMULATION 2:
THE COURTROOM

Trial lawyers practice their craft in simulated courtroom trials. Actors are often hired to play the roles in the simulated dramas because they are professional role players. Playing the roles of plaintiff, defendant, or witness, actors may find themselves under intense cross-examining by the prosecuting and defending attorneys (lawyers in training) or the judge. In the legal profession, where the performance of precise language determines success, practicing in the "moot court" is taken very seriously.

The courtroom simulation is simple to implement and facilitates much useful language practice and has, therefore, become a popular exercise for the language classroom. There are six roles providing parts for all students:

1. Defense attorney
2. Prosecuting attorney
3. Plaintiff
4. Defendant
5. Judge
6. Jury members

Teacher's Instructions

Tell students that there will be a courtroom trial to decide this case. Assign the roles to students and give the "actors" the appropriate role cards. Give actors time to read and think about their roles. The defendant and the defense attorney should review their cards together and discuss strategy. The plaintiff and prosecuting attorney do the same.

The rest of the students are the jury. During the trial, the jury is not allowed to speak. After the trial, the jury will discuss the situation and then vote on whether the defendant is guilty or not of theft and assault. The judge, lawyers, plaintiff, and defendant should listen to the jury but are not allowed to speak while the jury is discussing their verdict. Because the jury cannot speak during the trial, it is the responsibility of the judge to be sure that all points made by the defense and prosecution have been clear enough to be understood by the jury. The judge should feel free to ask the speakers to repeat or clarify any points they make. During the discussion by the jury, the others will discover the extent to which they have been understood by the jury and the amount of sympathy they have been able to instill in the jury.

Set up the courtroom by placing a table and chair at the front of the class for the judge. Also place one empty chair next to the judge's table for the other characters to sit in when they are "called to the stand."

After the verdict has been announced, the role playing is over. Answer questions the players might have about language, the legal system, and so forth. During the process you should take notes to be used during the discussion to recall points you want to make. Discuss problems students had in making themselves clear, arguing persuasively, and playing their roles.

This exercise can be repeated with other circumstances. With practice, students become more skilled at playing the roles and arguing effectively. You might choose a real court case or current issue of public concern to deal with in this manner. You could include news articles as background reading in preparation for a courtroom simulation.

Role Card 1:

Defense Attorney
Help your client prepare the defense by writing down the facts and thinking of all the things you will need to say in defense. You must convince the judge and jury that no crime has been committed. You are a young lawyer who is very clever. You need to win cases in order to become well known and popular. You do not like to lose cases because it hurts your career.

Role Card 2:

Prosecuting Attorney
Help your client (the woman) by thinking of all the facts of the case which need to be presented in court. Exactly what happened? Decide *how* you will tell the story to the judge so that your client wins. Try to show the jury that the young man violated the woman's freedom and that he is a thief.

　　You have been a lawyer for many years. You hate crime on the streets of this city and you would like to put all thieves in prison. You are friends with the judge because you went to law school with him/her.

Role Card 3:

Plaintiff
You were on the bus/subway/streetcar/etc., between _____ and
_____. You were going to work. It was very crowded and everyone was pushing. One young man was standing too close to you and he kept knocking into you with his newspaper in his arms. He even had the nerve to tell you to put out your cigarette. You didn't of course, because you were *not* in the no-smoking car. You ignored him because you don't think it is a good idea to talk with strange men when they bother you in public. Suddenly, the man grabbed the cigarette from your mouth and threw it down on the floor and stamped it out. When you saw his large hands in front of your face you screamed and when he stole your cigarette you yelled *thief*. Some fellow riders helped you by pulling the man away and holding him until the police came. You told the police that the man attacked you and stole your cigarette and they arrested him.

　　You are a sales clerk in a drugstore in a very busy part of the city. People are nasty to you when you are working and you don't like your job. Nobody cares enough to talk to you there, they just come in to buy newspapers, then they leave. You wish you had a more interesting job. Lately there has been a lot of crime in the streets around where you work and you are nervous when you go to work.

Role Card 4:

Defendant

You are on trial for theft and attacking a woman. One morning on the train, it was very crowded and you were forced to get into the smoking car. You had to stand with many other people, shoulder to shoulder. The woman standing in front of you had a new, freshly lit cigarette hanging from her mouth. Since all of the smoke was drifting straight into your face, you asked her to put it out. You were quite bothered by it because smoke makes your eyes sore and it's very bad for your breathing. Also, you were fresh and clean first thing in the morning and didn't want dirty smoke all over your clothes and in your hair. You asked the woman politely, but she replied by ignoring you and turning away. You then became angry and grabbed the cigarette from her, threw it onto the floor, and stamped it out. She reacted by screaming that you had attacked her and she also screamed "thief." Then, several large men grabbed you and held you at the next station until the police arrived.

This happened on the train between _____ and _____. You were arrested at _____. You are a student. You don't smoke and you don't drink very much. You jog daily and you think that physical health is very important. You have some very good friends who smoke but they would *never* smoke a cigarette in a crowded room.

Role Card 5:

Judge

You have been a judge for a long time. You are tired of hearing about growing crime in the streets and on public transportation. You want to put all criminals into prison. You feel that it is important for all people to feel free to walk the streets and not be afraid. You are very fair and feel that people's rights should be protected. You are friends with the prosecuting attorney because you went to school with him or her. You are the boss in your courtroom. You will:

1. Announce that "this court is in session."
2. Call the plaintiff to tell her story. Listen and give feedback if necessary. Be sure that the story is clear so that the jury understands it.
3. Then, call the defendant to tell his story.
4. Then, call the prosecuting attorney to clarify the prosecution's side of the story. He or she may call and interview the plaintiff, the defendant, or any witnesses.

5. Then, call the defense attorney to clarify the defense's story. He or she may call anyone he wants to the stand.

6. When everyone has told his story, thank the participants and say, "This court is in recess. The jury will now meet to decide the verdict."

Role Card 6:

Jury Members

You are a group of citizens chosen to sit on a jury. First, you must observe the trial. During the trial you are not allowed to speak. Then, you will have a jury meeting to discuss the situation with the other jurors. You must decide whether or not the defendant is guilty of *theft* and *assault* (attacking the woman with intent to harm her). In the discussion, listen carefully to the other jurors and let them help you form your opinion. Be sure to clearly present your own opinion to the others on the jury.

First, each member of the jury will give his or her opinion and explain the reason. Then, if the opinion is not unanimous, the jury will discuss their opinions in greater depth. An attempt should be made to reach a consensus. If, at the end of your discussion, you cannot announce a verdict of "guilty" or "not guilty," then announce that you are a "hung jury."

SIMULATION 3:
THE TUNNEL PROJECT

The following role-playing simulation is especially appropriate for training business people, or others needing practice in group cooperation, problem solving, brainstorming, moderation, and making presentations. There are two roles:

1. The entrepreneurs
2. The bankers

The role of the banker can be played by the teacher or else by a group of students. The bankers might not need as much time to prepare as the entrepreneurs do. It is best to have several competing groups of entrepreneurs with two or three members per group.

Reading Passage for "The Tunnel Project"

Hole in the Ground Inc.

For rent: two abandoned subway tunnels that stretch for nearly two miles some 50 feet beneath the streets of Manhattan. They are dark, dank and almost inaccessible. Present occupants are a few rats. If interested, contact New York's Metropolitan Transportation Authority.

Though the pitch was not phrased in exactly that way, the MTA did indeed offer last July to lease two vacant subway tunnels to "an imaginative entrepreneur." Now Vital Records Inc. of Raritan, N.J., thinks that it has enough imagination. The company, which stores financial records on computer tapes and microfilm for 50 of the largest U.S. corporations, proposes to convert the tunnels into a vast underground filing cabinet.

If its offer is accepted, the firm will have to install a computer-controlled file locator system and conveyor belts throughout the tunnels in order to turn them into a vault. Cost: an estimated $2 million. Despite those expenses, subterranean storage is expected to cost only $1 per sq. ft., compared with up to $50 per sq. ft. for aboveground space.

Reading Passage for All Participants

The property described in the article above is for sale, and several companies wish to take it over. A large bank is willing to provide financing for the new owners of the tunnel. The bank will help the new owners buy the tunnel, rebuild it in any way, and support the new business venture until it can support itself. The bank is offering loans of several million dollars: the exact amount will be negotiated between the bank and the new owners. There are several interested companies submitting proposals to the bank. In order to win the loan contract from the bank, a company must come up with the best, i.e., the most interesting, creative, potentially profitable, and feasible proposal for the use of the tunnel. The representatives of the winning company must also present their proposal professionally and convincingly.

Role Card 1:

The Entrepreneurs

1. You are partners in your own, very successful property development company. Meet with your business partners and develop a proposal for the tunnel project. Prepare a list of the basic points of your proposal. Also prepare to present and defend your proposal in a face-to-face meeting with the bank representative(s). Your proposal must be clear, convincing, and professional.

2. Present and defend your proposal. The bank will hear all competing proposals and award the loan contract to the company that presents the most convincing proposal. The bank will also consider the style and clarity of the presentations. You may listen as the other companies make their presentations, but do not interrupt.

3. Listen to, but do not participate in, the discussion of the bankers as they decide on the recipient of the financial support.

Role Card 2:

The Bankers

1. Meet to discuss criteria for choosing the company that will receive your support. Write a list of questions to ask the companies. Think about the criteria mentioned in the reading passage, which will influence your decisions. Be sure to apply these criteria in your decision making task.

2. Listen to the proposals and question the presenters very thoroughly.

3. After hearing all proposals, meet to choose the winner of the competition.

SCENE WORK

In your search for scenes to work on, do not hesitate to extract scenes from full-length plays. It is not necessary for the class to read an entire play in order to benefit from working on one scene.

The scene below is from Agatha Christie's one-act play called *The Patient*. This single scene can be easily introduced as classroom material. It is a very practical scene because it is short, and at the same time, it contains a good number of roles (five speaking roles), allowing many students to participate at once. The distribution of labor is equitable so that no student is required to tackle a large quantity of language, yet every student in the scene is involved in the action at every moment. The scene is interesting and lively, making it a pleasure to perform.

Instead of giving students a synopsis of this scene, I prefer to let them read it aloud several times and decide for themselves what is going on. I usually list the characters' names on the board and ask the students to explain who each one is and what the main motivations and functions of each one are within the scene. We then discuss the innuendo and possible background that is suggested in the scene. An alternative method for introducing a scene is to have students role play some of the beats of the scene before they read it. The role playing of each beat need not take long and should require little or no preparation. Use different students for each beat. See the beats from the scene below, for example.

THE PATIENT
by Agatha Christie

WINGFIELD: [*Moving to* EMMELINE] You keep saying she tried to commit suicide. I don't believe it. I won't believe it!

EMMELINE: [*With meaning*] She had plenty to make her depressed.

WINGFIELD: What do you mean by that?

EMMELINE: [*Rising*] I think you know quite well what I mean. I'm not blind, Bryan.

WINGFIELD: Jenny wasn't depressed. She'd nothing to be depressed about. You've got an evil mind, Emmeline, and you just imagine things.

ROSS: Leave my sister alone.

BRENDA: [*Rising and facing* EMMELINE] It was an accident. Of course it was an accident. Miss Ross is just trying to—trying to . . .

EMMELINE: [*Facing* BRENDA] Yes, what am I trying to do?

BRENDA: It's women like you that write anonymous letters—poison pen letters. Just because no man has ever looked at you . . .

EMMELINE: How dare you!

ROSS: [*Rising*] Oh, my God! Women! Cut it out, both of you.

WINGFIELD: I think we're all rather overexcited, you know. We're talking about things that are quite beside the point. What we really want to get at is, what was Jenny's state of mind on the day she fell? Well, I'm her husband, I know her pretty well, and I don't think for a moment she meant to commit suicide.

EMMELINE: Because you don't want to think so—you don't want to feel responsible!

WINGFIELD: Responsible? What do you mean by responsible?

EMMELINE: Driving her to do what she did!

ROSS: ⎫   ⎧ What do you mean by that?
WINGFIELD: ⎬ [*Together*] ⎨ How dare you!
BRENDA: ⎭   ⎩ It's not true!

GINSBERG: [*Rising*] Please—please! When I asked you to come here, it was not my object to provoke recriminations.

ROSS: [*Angrily*] Wasn't it? I'm not so sure. [*He wheels round and looks suspiciously at the* INSPECTOR]

GINSBERG: No, what I had in mind was to conduct an experiment.

BRENDA: We've already been told that, but you still haven't told us what kind of experiment.

GINSBERG: As Inspector Cray said just now—only one person knows what happened that afternoon—Mrs. Wingfield herself.

WINGFIELD: [Sighing] And she can't tell us. It's too bad.

EMMELINE: She will when she's better.

GINSBERG: I don't think you quite appreciate the medical position, Miss Ross. [He crosses to the electrical apparatus. BRENDA sits] It may be months—it may even be years before Mrs. Wingfield comes out of this state.

WINGFIELD: Surely not!

GINSBERG: Yes, Mr. Wingfield. I won't go into a lot of medical details, but there are people who have gone blind as a result of shock and have not recovered their sight for fifteen or twenty years. There have been those paralysed and unable to walk for the same periods of time. Sometimes another shock precipitates recovery. But there's no fixed rule. [To the INSPECTOR] Ring the bell, please.

[The INSPECTOR crosses and rings the bell below the doors]

An Incomplete List of Beats from a Scene from *The Patient*

Situation: Jenny Wingfield is critically injured after a mysterious fall from a balcony.

Beat 1: Emmeline claims that Jenny tried to commit suicide because she was depressed. Emmeline blames Jenny's husband for this. Jenny's husband does not believe his wife would try to harm herself, and he claims she had nothing to be depressed about. He accuses Emmeline of having an evil mind.

Beat 2: Brenda says Jenny simply had an accident. She accuses Emmeline of trying to cause trouble by writing anonymous letters about the Wingfield's marriage. Emmeline reacts defensively.

Beat 3: Wingfield asks everyone to calm down. He says it is important to think about Jenny's state of mind and denies she would try to commit suicide. Emmeline accuses Wingfield of being responsible for Jenny's fall. Wingfield defends himself.

Beat 4: Ross and Brenda demand to know why Dr. Ginsberg has gathered everyone together, if not to provoke recriminations. Ginsberg says his purpose is to conduct an experiment. He says Jenny might not wake up for a long time.

Preparing to Perform

As a supplement to scene work and role playing, you can practice the acting tasks that will be needed.

First, examine each character by asking the actors to think about how each character feels in the scene. Ask how "you" (the student) "would feel if you were the character." Develop a list of words to describe these feelings, for example: jealous, guilty, suspicious, loving, concerned, defensive, vindictive, overexcited, angry, inquisitive, analytical, indignant, horrified, disgusted, nervous, anxious.

To examine the language and behavior that are associated with these feelings and motivations, one or both of the following approaches can be taken.

The more "theatrical" action-oriented approach would be to have actors role play each item on the list. For example, the class stands in a circle. The teacher points to a student and calls out one word on the list. The student then immediately begins to "act" the word using both words and actions in a short spontaneous outburst. Each outburst last only about 30 seconds and is cut off when the teacher points to another student and calls out another word. This activity should be carried out at a quick and lively pace. Naturally, to be productive this requires a talent for spontaneity and imagination on the part of the students.

A more "intellectual" approach is to discuss the meanings of the words on the list. Describe situations that evoke these feelings, e.g., "One feels suspicious when . . . ," and actions that characterize these feelings, e.g., "When one is suspicious, one . . . ." Ask students to give examples of how each feeling is manifested in language and behavior.

Subtext

When working with scenes, examine the "subtext," or underlying meanings of the lines. Choose a few lines and discuss the subtext. Rewrite the lines to illustrate the subtext more directly. Remember to examine who is saying the lines and why. When students are familiar with the concept, have them analyze a scene in the same way. This makes a good group activity. An example is Emmeline's first line in the scene from *The Patient*

LINE: "She had plenty to make her depressed."

The subtext could be "You know very well that your wife was depressed about your affair with Brenda. I think you drove your wife to try to commit suicide so that you could get rid of her."

Role Playing the Background

Any scene can be used as a springboard for more role playing. After work on the Agatha Christie scene, students could role play situations suggested by the scene (See below).

Exercise

Step 1: In pairs, students are assigned situations based on the scene, which are created by the teacher or by the students themselves.

Step 2: Pairs work together to discuss a strategy for role playing and begin practicing. Ten to twenty minutes is enough.

Step 3: Each pair then role plays the situation for the class, expanding and developing what they have practiced. These should be loosely improvised scenes, not polished performances.

Step 4: (Optional) The class discusses the role playing and the implications of the actors' interpretations and compatibility of each role playing interpretation with the original scene or the synopsis of play.

With practice, students will become increasingly creative in their role playing. These types of exercises can be repeated throughout a language course using different scenes.

Sample Role Playing Situations

1. Emmeline and Bryan Wingfield, alone together, extend the argument that is based on the first four lines of the scene.

2. In their search for the person who might have tried to kill Mrs. Wingfield, Dr. Ginsberg and the police inspector discuss each of the other characters' potential as a suspect.

3. Ross apologizes for his sister Emmeline who has been implying that Brenda tried to kill Mrs. Wingfield because Brenda was having an affair with Mr. Wingfield. Ross explains how Emmeline never liked beautiful women (like Brenda). Brenda suddenly confesses to Ross that she has been having an affair with Mr. Wingfield, but that she did not do anything to Mrs. Wingfield. Brenda tells Ross that she is afraid that she will be blamed for Mrs. Wingfield's fall.

4. Brenda and Wingfield discuss their on-going affair and what they are going to do about it now that they are suspects in the attempted murder of Mrs. Wingfield.

5. Brenda and Wingfield are not having an affair and are discussing Emmeline's accusation that they are. They are both quite embarrassed by the whole thing and fear that it could blow out of proportion because of the attempted murder of Mrs. Wingfield.

Character Profiles

Class divides into at least two groups. A scene, such as the one above from *The Patient*, is distributed. Each group works independently to analyze the scene and its characters. Then each group creates a character profile of one or more of the scene's characters. This profile should include background which is not included in the scene but which is created by the students, as well as any information known about the character because of the scene. Background, personality and motivation of each character should be included.

The profiles from the groups (all based on the same character(s)) are compared. Any character features that are incompatible with the original scene should be noted and eliminated. Differences in character profiles are discussed.

Optional extension: Students create role-playing situations like those above for the purpose of contrasting profiles of the same characters. The situations, therefore, should be performed by as many pairs (or groups) of actors as there are profiles. The situations can be the same or different, but they should show the contrasts in profiles of the chosen characters.

Developing a Performance from a Scenario

Divide the class into teams, trios, or groups to develop scripts through improvisation from the beats of scenes. (See beats from *The Patient.*) Assign roles.

Instruct each student to begin by working alone to write some lines that will express his or her role and task within the scene. Since there is not much detailed information about each character, students are free to create their characters based on the information given in the scenarios.

Students meet with scene partners (working in pairs is the easiest) and work out dialogue, combining and blending lines and editing the scene so that both actors express their characters within the scene, and so the scene becomes a coordinated interaction. This task should be approached on the feet as an acting task with only minimal support from pen and paper. This is not merely a sit-down, brainstorming task. Students rewrite the scene together and practice it, working out bugs and developing ideas.

Teams present their scenes-in-progress to the class. You take notes. Direct the actors by making suggestions and having them repeat their scenes several times to incorporate the suggestions.

Work through the scenes in front of the class in order to help the actors develop their ideas. Attention to language and the expression of ideas is the focus of this stage. You should work with the actors to search for ideas. Pay less attention to what is wrong or right and more attention to what is possible.

Next, teams meet again to develop and practice ideas gained in the previous stage. Lines can be written and rewritten.

Finally, the actors perform again for the class. Use a tape recorder to review sections for discussion. Devote time to correcting the language. Convert successful scenes to script form as an option. Rewrite the scenario to fit the final performances and keep them for use in future classes.

Improvising a Scene

When working on any scene, play, or story, students need only a basic understanding of the story in order to begin role playing it. In the midst of other scene work, remove the scripts from the hands of your students and have them improvise the scene to the best of their ability. The initial improvisation of a scene can be very rough. Only an approximation of the actual text is necessary. Encourage the students to use their own words. Minute details can be glossed over and only the basic points of the scene emphasized. Different groups within the class should repeat the attempt. With each successive improvisation of the same scene, the scene should become more complete as the actors become more familiar with the basic structure.

A Scene Study Class

A scene study class is a constructive outlet for students' energies when there is time available to supplement regular language courses. In a scene study class, students work individually, in pairs, or in groups to develop performances of short scenes. These can be scenes from plays or they can be created by the participants themselves. A suggested format follows.

Step 1: Students work in groups on scenes. Each group works on a different scene. The teacher moves from group to group helping where necessary. Students work two to three hours or more on each scene.

Step 2: The class assembles to watch each group present its scene in whatever condition it is in. After each presentation, the teacher, audience, and actors criticize the scene making suggestions for further work. In addition, the teacher may "direct" students to replay various portions again, taking a modified approach or using some new techniques. For example, the teacher might make suggestions for improving pronunciation and hence the clarity of the scene, then ask the students to replay the scene incorporating the suggestions.

Step 3: Students work again in the same groups on the same scenes for several more hours, incorporating lessons learned in the performing/criticizing session.

Step 4: Finally, the scenes are performed and criticized again. Occasionally, throughout the above process, the teacher might assemble the class for an acting lesson or a language lesson. Clearly, some language and acting difficulties are shared by everyone.

There may be students who do not wish to act, but who wish to participate. These students can be used as directors or co-directors of scenes. The practice they get as "monitors" of the other students performances can be as useful to them as acting would be. It is helpful for the monitor to use a tape recorder to replay portions of the scenes that need comment or instruction.

It is sometimes useful to direct one group of actors through a scene using the rest of the students as monitors. Specific monitoring tasks can be assigned to each student, e.g., some can listen for intonation problems, others can monitor the non-verbal aspects, while others listen for vocabulary, grammar, and pronunciation problems.

Throughout the scene study process, the teacher should remember to adopt a low profile at times when students become involved in the task. The more the students themselves guide the entire process, the better.

There are anthologies of scenes from a variety of plays available in many bookstores. These scenes often must be adapted for the language classroom, but if the scenes are well written, it is worth the time it takes to adapt them. There are now, fortunately, a growing number of scripts that are actually written for the language classroom. Short scenes are recommended. Students can devote plenty of time to working on very short scenes. The longer the scene is, the more time it will take for the students to get beyond the "reading" stage and into the "acting" stage.

Scenes can be chosen to suit your needs. Sometimes it will be advantageous to have students working in twos and threes, and other times it will be helpful to have students working in larger groups. Short scenes with five to ten roles are useful when the director wishes to minimize the number of lines each actor must deal with, but maximize the material the actors have in common so as to facilitate class discussions.

Finally, scene study is a time-consuming process. There are no instant results, and one is advised to be patient and let the process take its course. There might be times when there seems to be no progress, or when the project seems too difficult. Such feelings are common, even among professional actors. Remember that the ultimate goal is to facilitate language practice and that the means is more important than the end result. Most likely, you and your students will be surprised at the quality of the end result.

Reader's Theater

I have found a reader's theater style to be especially adaptable to second-language courses with limited time. I particularly like the fact that almost any number of students can participate. The casting is flexible enough to accommodate unanticipated absences or additions to the cast. Also, because the parts are "read," students are not preoccupied with line memorization.

Any story written in a narrative style can be used. A short piece, lasting less than five minutes, can provide several hours of constructive class activity. One of my favorites is "A Unicorn in the Garden" from James Thurber's *A Thurber Carnival*, which is actually available in play script form.

For the performances of the story, students stand or sit on stools and hold their scripts in folders. Although lines are automatically memorized as a result of repeating the story in rehearsal, there is no pressure to memorize.

Some students are assigned character roles and some get narrator parts. Narrators can also play characters when they are not busy narrating. Simple costume pieces can be used to suggest characters. No scenery is necessary. As for the "acting," almost anything goes. As an added motivation, the finished product should be performed for an outside audience, for instance, another class, at a party, or some other gathering.

Variety Show

It may be easier than you think to organize an informal variety show in which your students perform for each other and their friends, or perhaps for some public function. Many students have performing talents that they can contribute to an evening of entertainment. Students are often pleased to be asked to share their native art. The best way to decide what to include in your variety show is to have the students themselves decide. At the University of Illinois there is an annual international fair that includes several evenings of songs, dances, and skits from many different countries. At The London School of English the students have informal evenings of coffee and conversation with performing by various students. One evening, a student from Belgium and another from Lebanon teamed up as a folk singing duet to play guitars and sing songs in English and their native languages. A Japanese banker surprised everyone with his finely polished rendition of "I Did It My Way," in Japanese! Students and teachers can also join together to perform skits. A popular and relatively easy addition to a variety show is the enacting of a series of jokes. Skits can be built around old and new jokes for the purpose of setting the audience up for the punchlines. Poetry readings are also ideal for variety shows. Students can find their own ways to bring the messages of the poetry to the audience. One approach that I recommend is to have one student reciting the poem in the original language, while another recites an English translation (contrapuntally), and with a third student playing guitar accompaniment.

As you have seen in this chapter, there is a wide variety of applications of the theater arts in language teaching. The possibilities certainly do not end here. You can enlarge your repertoire of teaching techniques by creating your own exercises. Your appreciation of the theater arts as a language teaching resource is only a beginning. As with any tool, we must learn how to use theater arts techniques in our language classrooms. A language teaching exercise takes on a life of its own each time a teacher and group of students uses it. It might change, taking on new forms when reused. It might take us time to develop or refine an exercise so that it fits our own teaching style. We must have the patience to learn through experience how best to apply what we have created.

Chapter 4

Play Production for Language Learning Groups: How to Organize and Direct Your Own Group

This chapter is included to illustrate how the techniques described in the preceding chapters can be incorporated into a full-fledged play production. It provides guidelines for language teachers wishing to direct their own plays in which language learners will be the performers. Written with the language teacher/novice director in mind, these guidelines provide the basic information necessary to get started. They are meant to be viewed as suggestions; teachers should adapt them to suit their own teaching conditions and artistic aims.

Whether with or without previous theater experience, teachers should find directing a play an enjoyable, artistic challenge, which is easier than one might imagine, and which is surprisingly productive in terms of language teaching. It is an experience that many teachers will want to repeat.

A CASE STUDY

So that the reader can benefit from actual experience, this chapter is written in the form of a case study of a performing theater group for language learners. This report deals with one successful production that was prepared and performed in one semester at the University of Illinois in Champaign-Urbana. Photos of another language learning theater group are included to

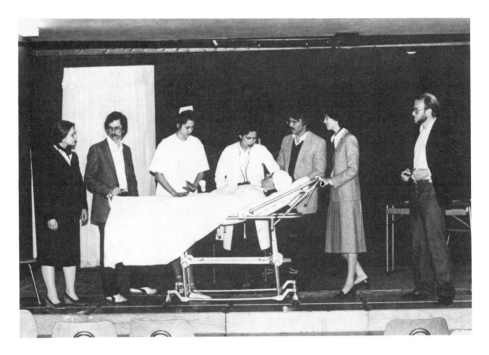

Theater in Englischer Sprache (TIES), a language learning theater group combining English learners and native speakers of English, in West Berlin, Germany, preparing to perform *The Patient*, by Agatha Christie. This production constituted a semester-long evening course in an adult education institute (Volkshochschule). Participants were members of the Berlin community interested in improving their English and/or learning about theater.

further illustrate the play production process. The photos show the group, called TIES, rehearsing for a production of Agatha Christie's one-act play, *The Patient*.

The "University of Illinois International Student Drama Group" (ISDG) was formed in the spring semester of 1981. It was an extracurricular group. Rehearsals were spread out over several months to coincide with the university semester with work beginning on February 1. During the last week in April Thornton Wilder's one-act play *The Long Christmas Dinner* was performed four times.

Getting Started

In order to begin, you will need (1) a play or scenes to perform, (2) language learners, and (3) time. Each of these factors will significantly affect the others, as you will see below. With each group of "actors" and each play you produce, the experience will be unique.

Before rehearsals can begin, you will need to do some preliminary planning: a play must be selected, actors must be recruited and/or matched with roles, space needs to be found for rehearsing and performing, an interested audience should be imaginable, performance dates (tentative if necessary) should be set, a general rehearsal schedule should be established (although kept flexible to adjust to your actors' needs), and the script must be interpreted to some extent.

Choosing the Play

One of the most important decisions you will make in organizing a theater group will be the selection of the play. The amount of time you have available will, of course, determine the length and complexity of the script you choose, as will the second language proficiency of your "actors." (See Recommended Readings and Classroom Material for script sources.)

I chose the play *The Long Christmas Dinner* by American playwright Thornton Wilder for several reasons. You may wish to consider them in choosing your plays.

1. It is short enough to handle—35 minutes running time. A new director might be surprised at the amount of time that can be spent in rehearsal working on a few lines or one single page. My advice is *keep it short!* *The Long Christmas Dinner* is 24 pages long, and that was plenty of material for us. It takes time to transfer the written text into living language.

2. The language is representative of the second language that the "actors" were learning, namely, American English. Although the language is a bit dated in places, it is a good example of spoken English. I also had to consider the level of difficulty of the language in relation to the learners' English proficiency. Most of the language in the script involves interaction between family members; furthermore, it is realistic language. From the beginning, most of the sentences were easy for the actors to understand. Since the vocabulary was understood by the actors at an early stage, we had time to work on the interpretation of the text.

   Another consideration was to choose a script containing language that the learners could use outside of the theater. I would have rejected the script if it had contained:

- highly stylized language, e.g., Shakespeare, or language that is abstract to the point of being unrealistic. (Some directors might wish to use scripts like Shakespeare or Moliere, especially when the learners have an interest in literature.)

- inappropriate dialects, e.g., those which are never or rarely heard in the area in which the students were living, or those containing too much non-standard grammar, obscenity, or obsolete slang.

- inappropriate subject matter, e.g., any subject matter that would have been difficult or impossible for the actors or audience (both groups consisting largely of foreign students and families) to relate to or that might have been offensive.

3. It is an excellent culture teaching tool because the story is a representative slice of American family life containing history, tradition, attitudes, and values, all of which change over time.

4. The acting skills required by the play were within the range that one could expect of amateur actors. No acts in the play demanded highly specialized performing skills or particularly low levels of inhibition.

5. There are a number of equally important roles so the distribution of labor is equitable. No actor has too much of the load to carry, or too little.

6. The roles are such that some actors can play several roles; the actors with the "small roles" can play other roles as well. As a result, everyone felt an important part of the play. This facilitates ensemble building. It also allows the director flexibility in casting. If 12 actors are available, the play can accommodate all of them, but if only 8, or even 6 are available, the show can still be produced. A small cast, however, is easier to handle than a large cast; the problems and conflicts of each individual actor are also the problems and conflicts of the director; the fewer actors there are, the fewer scheduling problems there are.

7. The technical demands of the play, i.e., set, props, sound, lighting, costumes, etc. are simple and inexpensive.

8. The rights to the production were available for a relatively small price. Royalty information and script prices were obtained by calling the publisher—Samuel French Inc., N.Y., N.Y. Scripts were ordered in the same phone call and arrived in the mail C.O.D. within a week. Royalties were $10.00 per performance payable one week before opening night.

The Actors

Students of English with a "low-intermediate" level of proficiency can successfully perform in English. The lower the level of the students' English, the simpler and perhaps shorter the material to be performed should be. For *The Long Christmas Dinner*, the students ranged from intermediate to advanced, e.g. some had not quite attained TOEFL (Test of English as a Foreign Language) scores high enough to be admitted to the university, some had been admitted but were taking remedial English courses, and others had been university students (in Illinois) for over one year.

Two of the eight actors were native speakers of English. The Americans were included in the cast because they provided good linguistic models and resources for the foreign students, as well as increased incentive for foreign student participation. Several students had indicated that they would be especially interested in working in the drama group if Americans, i.e., native speakers, would also be involved. After spending a semester or more in the university's Intensive English Institute, where everyone except the teachers is a foreigner, most of the students were eager to interact with Americans. The Americans did not, however, have the largest roles in the play, and they did not attend as many rehearsals as the non-native speakers of English since they obviously were not in as much need of language help. Although native speakers are a nice addition to such a drama group, and should be included when possible, their participation is not essential to the success of the venture.

The Time Commitment

A text, or script must be chosen to fit the time available. If only two weeks are available, for example, with only three hours scheduled each week, then a short sketch or scene will be ample. Students can learn a great deal by working on a piece that takes only two or three minutes to perform. One of my classes prepared a piece lasting about three minutes in approximately eight hours spread over two weeks. This was not an intensive schedule.

We spent nearly an entire semester producing *The Long Christmas Dinner*. We started the first week of February and rehearsed Monday, Tuesday, and Wednesday for two hours after dinner each evening, and on some Sunday afternoons for two hours. During two of the weeks, we did not meet at all, due to holidays. We spread our rehearsals over a period of three months to allow for a flexible schedule. We could have produced this play in half that time, but it would have required a more intensive rehearsal schedule.

Since this was an extracurricular activity, I explained to each actor individually, when casting, what the play would be, what his or her role would be, and what the time commitment would be. It was understood that, occasionally, individual actors would need to miss scheduled rehearsals because of academic pressure caused by tests, projects, and so forth, and that the play was not to be allowed to interfere with academic performance. At the same time, it was made clear that the play would be time consuming and hard work, and that a commitment by each individual was essential. During the middle of the rehearsal period it was often possible for me to schedule our work so that everyone did not need to be at every rehearsal.

The Space

In order to rehearse, we needed a rehearsal "space," or room. We rehearsed in a large university classroom with moveable furniture. We used chairs, table, and a few props at the beginning to represent the environment of the play. It is not necessary to work on the actual set or in the performance space until the last few weeks of rehearsal. The actors are so busy learning their roles that they do not have time to make use of the finishing touches of the environment until later. The rehearsal space should be close enough in size to the performance space so that, visually and acoustically, the transition to the theater will not be too disruptive to the development of the play.

Our performance space was the chapel of a small church. With its dark wood interior, high peaked ceiling, raised altar area complete with a huge pipe organ, and subdued stained glass windows, the space was an ideal setting for the play. In mood, the chapel is not unlike the interior of the Bayard home, the home in which the action of the play is set.

Plays can be performed anywhere. It is not necessary to find a theater in order to perform a play. Many plays actually are more effective in non-conventional spaces. The Off-Off Broadway theater movement in New York City and the Council of Off-Loop Theaters in Chicago consist of hundreds of small, frequently low-budget theater companies that perform in renovated store fronts, attics, and other non-conventional spaces. Outdoor theater can also be a very rewarding experience, weather permitting. Of course, a theater that is already a theater is convenient in that many of the necessities, stage lights for example, are already there.

The main considerations for choosing a space are: Will the audience and actors fit into the space? Will the audience be able to see and hear? Will the group have access to the space for rehearsals at least one or two weeks before the performances? Will the area be free of interference from other activities, during performance, for example, rock bands, parties, noisy meetings, street noise, the movement of people within the building, etc.

Props and Sets

For best results, choose a play that does not require elaborate sets and props. Some styles of theater use few or no sets and props, and therefore, all concentration is on the acting. Realistic settings, e.g., home interiors, offices, pubs, etc., are convenient because all set pieces and props can usually be gathered from the resources of the cast.

The Long Christmas Dinner required only a "representative," or partial, set; the props consisted mainly of table settings. We had a real dinner table, for example, and real place settings, but no food was used. All of the eating was pantomimed. This in accordance with Wilder's recommendations (Wilder 1934). Using real food would have been nearly impossible because of the demands of the play. We also avoided the task of finding props (or rather people) that could represent newborn babies by having the actors carry dolls wrapped in blankets. The bundles seemed to be real because of the way in which the other characters interacted with them. (This is the key to much good theater. Often it is not important for an object or situation to be real. The reality is perceived by the audience due to the way the actors react to the object or situation.)

When designing our set, we had to consider the logistics of our rehearsal situation. Since we were guests in our rehearsal and performance spaces, we had to carry the set and props in and out every day from some other location. Thus, our set had to be portable and easily assembled.

When gathering set pieces and props, the director should not hesitate to look to the community as a resource. Local merchants will often loan or donate a prop to the play. All performance programs should have a "special thanks" section for acknowledging such support. (See our program at the end of this chapter.)

For our play, most of the sets, props, and costumes came from the possessions of the cast. Wigs were loaned free of charge by a local hairdresser, a military uniform was loaned by the university's ROTC department, a cane was donated by a local merchant dealing in orthopedic products, and some costumes were loaned to us by a local community theater.

Lights

The lights, like the set, do not need to be complex. If the space is small, only a few are necessary. We were lucky because our space already had a few stage lights in it, but they were primitive—spot light bulbs mounted inside coffee cans, hung from the ceiling with c-clamps, and pointed toward the stage. One red, one blue, and three white bulbs were all that were necessary in this small space. Since there was no theatrical lighting control board, there were no light changes during the show except at the very beginning and at the end. The audience received a signal that the show was starting when the house lights went off. The stage lights were turned off shortly thereafter, just long enough for the actors to enter. Then they were turned back on. The only other light cue was at the end of the applause after the play, when the house lights were turned on again.

Sound

Music is an effective addition to a play, and its inclusion is a good way to expose the cast to some of the second culture's music. We included examples of "American" musical culture in *The Long Christmas Dinner*, not necessarily in the sense of music composed by Americans, but in the sense of music enjoyed by Americans.

For "Christmas dinner," we used traditional Christmas carols for pre-show music, which began twenty minutes before the beginning of the play. A World War II era jazz number highlighted the scene in the middle of the play in which Sam Bayard, age 18, marches off to fight and die in that war. "Silent Night" was used to underscore the mood of the closing scene in which the elderly aunt is finally left by her relatives to spend Christmas in the big old house alone. The post-show music consisted of more traditional Christmas carols, and it was played as the audience left the theater.

All the music we used was recorded onto tape from records, and played back on basic home stereo equipment. The only cost for sound was the cost of the blank cassette.

Interpreting the Script

Before meeting with the actors, you will need to interpret the script to some extent. You will be making discoveries about the play throughout the rehearsal process, so the initial interpretation will be subject to modification and expansion. Some of your future decisions regarding script interpretation will result from your unique production situation, that is, they will be creations of you and your cast, working together. In the beginning, though, you should do the following. Read the play several times, getting to know the story. Make a list of the characters and write out basic character descriptions for each. You might want to give these to the cast at some point. Think about the motivations, personalities, and backgrounds of the characters as well as the relationships between characters. Think about the setting(s) for the play, both in terms of time, geographic location, and set (e.g., home, forest, street, etc.). What is the style of the play? Is it realistic or absurd? Modern or historical? Comedy or drama? Is it an allegorical piece or a straightforward, what-you-see-is-what-you-get story? What are the main events?

You should mark the "beats" (see Chapter 2) of the play in your script. Make a list of beats for the actors. This can be modified later when more discoveries are made in rehearsal. Describe each beat in terms of the function of each scene. The beats you list will reflect your own interpretation of the play. For purposes of organization, some directors have the cast number the beats in their scripts so that they can be referred to in rehearsal. Rehearsal schedules can be organized according to beats: e.g., Monday: beats 1-3, Tuesday: beats 4-7, Wednesday: beats 1-7, etc. Below is the list of beats we used for *The Long Christmas Dinner*.

List of Beats

1. The first Xmas dinner in the new house.
2. The sixth Xmas dinner in the house.
3. Mother Bayard dies.
4. The next Xmas dinner, without Mother Bayard—a cold dark Xmas day.
5. Charles is born to Lucia and Roderick. The firm is young.
6. The next Xmas. An overcast day.
7. Genevieve is born.
8. The firm has a new factory!!! The family is growing wealthy. Talk is of the future.
9. Roderick is becoming very ill because of his drinking problem. He almost dies.
10. Roderick rejoins the family for the first Xmas dinner in years.
11. Charles replaces Roderick as the head of the household. Lucia, who is beginning to age fast, reminisces about the past.
12. Genevieve joins family for Xmas.
13. Roderick becomes very ill and dies.
14. One year later, Lucia reminisces about the past more and more.
15. Charles' romance with Leonora is revealed. Lucia is very depressed about the loss of Roderick, her children, and the structure of her family life.
16. Charles brings home his wife, Leonora.
17. Leonora replaces Lucia as female head of household. The first Xmas dinner in the home of Charles and Leonora. (same house)
18. A year later, Charles' and Leonora's baby is born and dies.
19. A later Xmas. Ermengarde is discussed. Brandon becomes ill. Lucia becomes ill.
20. Brandon dies.
21. Lucia dies.
22. A later Xmas. Sam and Lucia II are born. Genevieve's psychological condition worsens.
23. Dinner resumes. Talk is of the past, the age of the house, and Ermengarde.
24. Roderick Jr. is born.
25. Ermengarde arrives. Talk of family tree.
26. Sam departs for war.

27. Sam dies in the war in Europe.

28. The next Xmas. Talk of Sam.

29. Roderick Jr. and Charles ruin Xmas dinner by arguing. Roderick leaves home.

30. Lucia leaves home to marry.

31. A later Xmas. A beautiful day. Talk of Mrs. Foster. A telegram arrives from Lucia and her husband.

32. A later Xmas. A dark day. Charles is aged significantly. Genevieve breaks down.

33. A later Xmas. Ermengarde and Charles are sick.

34. Charles dies.

35. A later Xmas. Leonora and Ermengarde celebrate Xmas together. Leonora tells Ermengarde she is leaving.

36. Ermengarde celebrates Xmas alone.

37. Ermengarde dies happily.

Finally, you will need to think about the resources and acting skills needed to produce the play. You might decide to cut certain parts of the play before you start in order to make the actors' task easier or more practical. If, for example, the script calls for tap dancing or singing, and you do not have the talent available, or if it calls for explosives, live horses, or the use of what you consider to be unacceptable amounts of profanity or difficult language, then it might be possible to change the script. Directors often cut and modify scripts to shorten plays or to make them more practical. Cuts can also be made later if rehearsals reveal that particular sections are going to be too difficult to perform. (*Remember*: Significant changes may require the author's or publisher's permission.)

THE REHEARSAL PERIOD

Rehearsal Objectives

Below is an outline of our basic rehearsal objectives.

First meeting: read through
cast meets
discuss project

Early rehearsals: building the ensemble
learning the play (story, functions, lines, blocking)
actors' training begins (character study, physical and verbal expression: see exercises in Chapter 3; see also Chapter 2)

Middle rehearsals: character study and development
physical vocabulary
voice work
emotional vocabulary
tempo and rhythm

Later rehearsals: preparing to perform
performance ritual

Early Rehearsals

The early rehearsal period is when the individuals must be developed into a cooperative ensemble. For amateurs, the early rehearsal period is also a time of learning about the theater process. In addition, these rehearsals must revolve around learning about the play. It is up to the director to be sure that all three of these objectives are being met at the same time.

It is important to realize that the whole drama process is an ensemble-building process. By the time the play is ready for performance, the actors should form a friendly and cooperative group. At first, though, the group may seem competitive and even incompatible. All members have their own individual reasons for being in the group, and if they all set out to achieve their own goals individually, conflict may result.

It is up to the director to be sure that the group works together. Everyone should understand the goals of the group and how those goals are to be accomplished, that is, systematically, over time, according to the director's scheme. It is made clear that everyone is going to be given tools with which to learn to act and develop a role. The actors are put at ease with the knowledge that they are not expected to simply begin acting artfully from the start. They will be taught. At the same time, they must learn to let themselves be directed. The director's first task, then, is to secure the actors' trust.

When working with non-native speakers of English who are untrained actors, the progress of the cast is slower than it would be if everyone were a native English speaker already familiar with the theater process. Not recognizing that they are passing through the same stages of development that every cast must pass through, and not realizing at first the difficulty of each stage of the rehearsal process, novice actors may become discouraged. The director must at all times be demanding and display unlimited faith in the ability of the cast to reach its goal. The director must at all times maintain a high level of energy and interest in rehearsal, always watching every move the actors are making on stage, no matter how slow their progress; the director must pour inspiration into the actors. Results will come, but faith is a necessary ingredient.

When observing students in rehearsal, it is important to remember that the quiet or "stiff" actors are not necessarily "bad" actors or in any way unfit for the task. Teachers are advised not to panic upon realizing that the student

with the largest role seems to be the least talented. Often the least spontaneous students turn out to be the best: Many people simply require time to
ease into the role of "actor." Actors should be encouraged, but not pushed,
into their roles. There is much to think about when creating a role and
naturalness does not necessarily come first. As a director you must resist the
temptation to give your actors too much direction at one time. Isolate problems and work on them one at a time. Above all, be patient. This process
takes time.

Instead of casting a play before rehearsals begin, some directors prefer to
spend the early rehearsals learning about the play and the actors and molding
the group into an ensemble while, at the same time, forming an opinion as to
which actor should play each role. This method gives the director time to
observe the actors at work before matching them with their roles. If you
choose this method of casting you would spend the early rehearsals reading,
discussing, and role playing the characters while rotating actors from role to
role in order to observe each actor playing different roles. As soon as possible,
the casting decisions should be made so that the actors can begin developing
their characters.

First Rehearsal

Our first rehearsal was simply a read through. This means that we sat down
and read the play aloud. No acting was necessary or desired, since it was too
early to begin making decisions about characterization. Sitting comfortably
in my living room and drinking coffee, the actors were introduced to each
other and the play. We also reviewed the schedule and talked about what the
rehearsals would be like. After the reading, we discussed the play in order to
clarify the basic story. It may not always be possible or desirable to meet in
the director's home. The rehearsal space, be it classroom, theater, or intermediate location, could be used for the first meetings, too. The important
thing is for the atmosphere to be as relaxed and informal as possible. The
sooner the members of the group feel comfortable together, the better!

First Weeks

The first week of rehearsal started with a second read through with more
questions asked. After that, we began working on our feet with the play,
even though the actors were still unsure of the meaning of much of the
vocabulary and many of the lines. In the beginning, it is important that the
play does not become too intellectualized; in order to foster spontaneity, the
actors should learn about the play actively by speaking and walking through
it. While the acting will sound and look unnatural at first, it is important to
remember that native English-speaking actors go through the same stages in
rehearsal.

I used some basic acting lessons, games, role playing, and group warm-
ups to help my cast form an ensemble. The exercises we did in early rehearsals
together helped the actors to get to know each other and begin to feel at ease.

These included many of the voice and body warm-ups and exercises listed in previous chapters: circle warm-ups, like, "Pass the Poem," "Squeeze Play," "Pass the Body," "Drop the Box" (Chapter 3), "Cup Ball," "Economy in Acting" (Chapter 2), and so forth.

The role playing involved scenes both from the script and from the lives of the play's characters as we imagined them. Simple interactions between characters in the play were role played. For example, we enacted a scene in which the son, Roderick, asks his mother, Lucia, for permission to stay out late at night, although no such scene is in the play. This helped the actors to begin forming ideas about the nature of the mother–son relationship that Roderick and Lucia have. It also provided the opportunity to discuss the cultural elements of such an interaction in American settings characteristic of both present and past generations.

In the first week of rehearsal, we warmed up and did acting exercises for 30 to 45 minutes at the beginning of each rehearsal before beginning to work on the script. The vocal warm-ups had to be taught, of course, in the beginning. These warm-ups are much like pronunciation drills but they have a more immediate purpose. Warm-ups help actors become comfortable working in front of their colleagues. Although the actors may feel self-conscious

Physical Warm-ups, *The Patient*: The warm-up session begins with light physical warm-ups which relax and stimulate the actors.

Group Vocal and Physical Warm-ups, *The Patient*: Listening and watching mechanisms are warmed up as the actors coordinate sound and movement for an ensemble effect.

the first few times through the warm-ups, they will eventually relax when they realize that they are not going to be asked to do anything more outrageous than flex their voices. It is somehow easier than singing, and no one is required to do it on key or solo; it is a group task. Eventually, a group begins to make productive use of warm-up time, and the actors really relax and flex their voices. Besides exploring their vocal ranges, actors use warm-ups to get used to manipulating their voices in front of other actors, and they alleviate fears about how fellow actors may react if they experiment with their voices in rehearsal. People who can stand in a circle and warm-up their voices together will not be likely to feel uncomfortable doing other new things together. In the meantime, the actors learn to manipulate the vocal instrument, which is a valuable skill in any language learning situation. (See Chapter 3 "The Voice," and "The Body.")

Blocking

In the first week of rehearsals "blocking" can begin. Blocking is the technical aspect of coordinating stage movement. The director "blocks" the play by deciding where the actors will be located for each scene in the play, and how and where they will move from one position to another. Blocking can be either totally in the hands of the director, or the director can simply give the actors an idea of what the set will look like, and then, through suggestions, let the actors develop the blocking themselves as rehearsals progress. It is often best to give the actors as much freedom in movement as possible. The best alternatives for blocking often evolve out of the ongoing rehearsal process. In the beginning I recommend guiding the actors enough to make them reasonably comfortable, and to see that they actually use the set in a balanced and effective way. Remember that initial blocking is only to get the actors moving within a defined space, and that blocking can and should be changed as the group discovers new and better possibilities. Actors usually are not prevented from changing their blocking when they wish, except when a change in blocking interferes with some other actor or the effectiveness of some stage "business." Until the very end, the director should watch for situations in which the blocking is interfering with the effective execution of any part of the play. Common symptoms of problematic blocking are (1) the actor(s) cannot be heard, (2) the actor(s) cannot be seen, (3) the actors are very uncomfortable, and (4) they find it difficult to execute some business.

Since the complete set for the play usually is not ready at the beginning of the rehearsal period, the floor plan of the set is sometimes taped onto the floor so the actors can get used to the dimensions of their performing area. In any case the actors should see at least a rough drawing of the set so they can envision it as they work.

Directors usually divide the play into sections and block one or two sections at a time, giving the actors the time to run through each section several times so that they can begin to learn their blocking. Actors should write their blocking into their scripts so that it is not forgotten. Single words and abbreviations are helpful when writing down blocking, e.g., "xdl" = cross down left, "exit usl" = exit up stage left, etc. Actors can create their own system of shorthand for recording blocking. Other helpful words are: stand, sit, exit, enter, laugh, cry, turn, look, drink, run, faint, etc. The standard stage directional vocabulary is included with the set illustration below.

stage left	sl
stage right	sr
up stage	us
down stage	ds
center stage	cs
up stage left	usl
down stage center	dsc

```
                    ┌─────────────────────────────┐
                    │            us               │
                    │                             │
                    │ sr        cs            sl   │
                    │                             │
                    │            ds               │
                    └─────────────────────────────┘
                               audience
```

Blocking rehearsals are an opportunity for the actors to get to know the play and each other before actually beginning to develop three-dimensional characters. At this point it is not necessary for them to be "acting" totally as their characters would act. After all, they probably do not know enough about their characters to do that yet.

A Typical Rehearsal

An outline for a typical rehearsal follows. Although rehearsals differ from day to day, most rehearsals are based on the outline or some portions of it. The earlier rehearsals are characterized by more exercises and working through the script. The later rehearsals are characterized by more spot rehearsals, i.e., the quick fixing of problem areas, and run-throughs with few or no stops.

Early Rehearsals, *The Patient*: In the early stages of rehearsal, the actors are dependent on their scripts as they learn their roles. The action will be slow and even mechanical at times as they lay the basic ground-work for future, more spontaneous rehearsing.

Basic Rehearsal Plan

Starting rehearsal

greeting the actors, chatting, setting up, announcements; always establishing a friendly atmosphere, the director greets each actor individually, establishing that each is fine and ready to work.

Warming up

1. making individuals into an ensemble
2. warming-up the individual's equipment

Working on the script

1. false starts in which the actors are still warming-up
2. stop and go
3. run-through
4. notes
5. work through problem sections
6. run-through
7. notes

At first, run-throughs will consist only of a series of sections of the script. Later, run-throughs will consist of the entire show.

The Middle Rehearsals

Once the actors begin to be comfortable with the blocking, the basic story, and each other, they are ready to start building their characters and orchestrating their performances. That is, they will be filling in all the missing pieces and rehearsing until a smoothly flowing play is developed. The director must now focus the actors' attention on character development. At this stage in rehearsal, all of the actors' language skills come into play (see especially Chapter 2). The actors must learn to understand their characters and learn to feel, think, and act like their characters.

This stage of rehearsal should be characterized by experimentation on everyone's part. The actors should experiment with tones of voice, different stress and intonation patterns, emotional and physical vocabulary, character interpretation, and so forth. The director should also be experimenting with the play at this point. You must find ways to highlight the important moments and events in the script (the beats) through blocking, line deliveries, and the non-verbal behavior of the characters.

It is helpful to give the actors the list of beats, if you have not already done so, and rehearse each beat as a separate self-contained unit when necessary. At times, you will want to stop and start the actors many times to get them comfortable in the execution of only a few lines. At other times, you will simply watch to see what develops, allowing the actors to muddle through on their own. Work on the script must be continually interspersed with warm-ups, role playing, games, and discussions in order to focus the cast's attention and energies in productive directions. Do not forget to break away from the script to teach the cast skills that will help them with the play, e.g., pronunciation, vocal projection, tempo, listening, non-verbal acting, sense memory, substitution, and so forth. In addition, do not be afraid to break away from the script for a significant period of time in order to role play or discuss aspects of the play that require a deeper understanding. You should get your actors to think about answers to questions like, "How would I feel if . . ." in order to help them see the story through the eyes of their characters.

We enhanced our understanding of the relationships between characters in *The Long Christmas Dinner* by asking questions such as the following. How does Roderick feel when his mother dies? Why isn't Charles sadder when his mother dies? What type of relationship do cousins Brandon and Roderick have in the firm they both work in? How did Roderick meet his wife? Answers to questions can be found in several places. Some answers are in the script, e.g., How old is the daughter, Genevieve, when she finally leaves home? Some answers are generated as a result of decisions the ensemble makes, e.g., should the son, Charles, react with a sense of humor when teased by his mother and sister about being engaged, or should he be irritated and defensive? Other answers are dictated by the director, e.g., I decided to have the war in which the son, Sam, dies be WWII instead of WWI as Wilder originally intended. This moved the time span of the play 25 to 30 years closer to the present.

Finally, although the actors need consistency from the director in order to feel comfortable and secure in their roles, there are many changes you will want to make as your play unfolds. Each play with its own cast, script, and circumstances is a unique production, and many of the finer elements of your production will emerge only from the process itself. You cannot anticipate everything, nor should you try to.

Line Memorization

Do not worry about line memorization. Students usually find it easy to remember their lines after so much intensive work on a script. In fact, many times, students remark that it took them no extra effort to memorize their lines: they simply learned them from rehearsing. Early in rehearsals you can surprise your actors by asking them to play a scene or two without scripts. They may feel that they do not know the scene well enough, but tell them to "fake it" as best they can. Everyone will be surprised when the students are able to play the scene with many of the actual lines spoken correctly. Remember, the correct lines are not as important as the action of the play. To give the actors a feel for the structure of the play you might ask them to role play the entire play after only a few rehearsals using only the list of beats as a reference.

Approximately midway through your rehearsal period you should begin to wean the actors from their scripts. They will find it much easier to "act" when they are not holding, and looking at, their books. You might want to specify a particular rehearsal, announced two weeks in advance, as the first run-through "off-book," that is, without scripts. During this run-through, actors may stumble a bit, but you will probably be surprised (and so will they) at how well they know their lines. Someone who is not acting should watch the book during the first few off-book rehearsals and prompt the actors when necessary. Instruct your actors to call out the single word "line" when they are in need of prompting: When a line or cue is forgotten, actors should call "line" as often as they need to, but they should *never* break concentration. Encourage them not to apologize or demonstrate frustration over forgotten

Middle Rehearsals, *The Patient*: In the middle stages of the production period the actors become less dependent on the written text, and are, therefore, more able to focus their attention on extra-linguistic elements such as stress and intonation, gesture, proxemics, eye contact, posture, physical tension, etc.

lines when they are supposed to be acting. During the playing of a scene, the only word that should be allowed, other than those of the characters, is "line." With a few rehearsals to go before the first performances, actors should be discouraged (or forbidden) to call for lines. In the performances, actors will have to improvise if they forget lines, and they should get accustomed to doing so.

Video

Video taping sessions can highlight actors' acting problems so that they know where to focus their attention in future rehearsals. Watching the video tape, the actors learn about how inconsistencies in individual and ensemble work affect the performances. Make a number of takes of one scene, so that the actors can view each take and then attempt to improve their performance for the subsequent takes. If necessary, use a warm-up exercise between two of the takes to help the actors reach a higher energy level. You can accomplish this with a "line speed-through," an exercise in which the actors sit and speak the lines aloud as fast as possible without pauses. The difference between the take before the line speed-through and the take after it is often significant. Also, if the first take is difficult to understand (the actors will agree with you on this point upon viewing the tape), put the cast through some vocal warm-ups that focus on articulation. The next take should be significantly clearer.

We made a video tape of one scene from *The Long Christmas Dinner*. We chose the scene which, at the time, was in the best condition in terms of the acting. Although the actors felt confident (overconfident) regarding their ability to perform this particular scene, the video tape revealed a multitude of flaws in their acting. The actors concluded that they were not being specific enough in setting their actions. They had made many correct decisions in analyzing the scene, but at that point they were still having problems communicating their decisions to the audience.

All of the problems that were revealed by the video tape could be described as language problems. For example, one of the most urgent problems was a lack of clarity of speech. Although the actors were strong and confident in their line delivery, the performance was almost incomprehensible. We analyzed the problems: articulation was unspecific and careless, the tempo was too fast, vowels were too clipped, stress was misplaced, words and phrases were swallowed (mumbled), volume was too low, pauses were too long and were misplaced, facial expressions were inconsistent with character, and physical expression was forced and, at times, inappropriate.

Last Rehearsals

In this later stage of rehearsals it is important for the cast to experience the play as it will be performed. This means that all things should be "set," that is, as soon as possible, everything should be as it will be in performance, and few changes should be made.

The addition of the final costume pieces, set pieces, props, and technical effects, such as light and sound, should be made far enough in advance so that unanticipated changes caused by these new elements can be assimilated comfortably by the cast. The director can then be free to make any changes that the new elements demand, without putting the cast in the uncomfortable position of having to adapt to new aspects in front of the audience. It takes several run-throughs for the cast to get used to moving in their costumes, handling new props, listening for new sound cues, e.g., music, and playing the lights.

Another reason that the dramatic action should be set before the beginning of these technical rehearsals is that the technical rehearsals are full of distractions that prevent much attention from being devoted to new acting problems. The director can help the cast at this point by preparing for rehearsals so that the addition of technical elements runs smoothly, and the flow of the show is only interrupted temporarily. The cast needs to experience as many smooth runs of the complete show as possible before the audience comes. Clumsy technical rehearsals can introduce awkward tempos and rhythms into the show.

Run-throughs

We began complete nonstop run-throughs with five full weeks (three or four rehearsals per week) left to go before opening night. Rehearsals during this period alternated between run-throughs and work-throughs, i.e., stop-and-go rehearsals. As often as possible, I would let the actors run through the show without being stopped. This experience is important because it lets them get used to the tempos and rhythms of the show. It is easy to forget how fast the play moves when the director constantly stops and reworks scenes.

Typically, in the last month, we would work through the entire play for the first half of a rehearsal. Then we would have at least one nonstop run-through. In the last few weeks of the rehearsal period, we had several rehearsals in which we did two run-throughs. Between run-throughs, I gave the cast notes, and then I watched to see that the instructions were incorporated into the next run-through. Any instructions that proved too difficult to assimilate in the second run-through could be worked into the performance in the next work-through.

Invited Rehearsal Audiences

During the last three weeks, I occasionally invited one or more outsiders to observe rehearsals. This adds a great deal of energy to the rehearsals because the cast members feel that they are really "performing" the piece. They sense a need to communicate the play to someone who, unlike the director, does not already know the story. Observers in rehearsal also give the cast experience in dealing with their nervousness. All actors get nervous and excited in front of an audience, especially in the first performances of a play. What experienced actors know is that nervousness is normal and, with practice, they will be able to control their nervous energy.

In addition to periodically inviting one or more observers to rehearsal, the director should arrange to have entire audiences at the last two or three rehearsals. The larger the audience for these rehearsals, the better. Invited dress rehearsals give the actors a chance to perform the play in its final form in front of whole audiences, before they have to do it for the paying public. Mistakes will happen in front of these audiences. The cast needs to learn that mistakes are commonplace, and that they are not to be regarded as failures. If handled well, most mistakes will not come to the attention of the audience. More mistakes are bound to happen in the first performances, because the cast's energy levels are quite high, and often a bit out of control. Each actor must deal not only with his or her own nervous energy, but with that of the rest of the ensemble. One's fellow actors can become unpredictable when they suddenly find themselves before an audience. A solution to this problem is to have invited audiences in dress rehearsals. The audience should be aware that they are invited to a final dress rehearsal, rather than a performance. This allows the director to stop the performance, if necessary, to make repairs—although such stops should be avoided if possible. Groups, such as classes, clubs, and organizations are good sources of invited audience members: only one invitation can secure a substantial number of audience members. Interested friends and colleagues also make sympathetic viewers. The invitation can be directed so as to avoid stealing potential audience members from the official public performances.

The ISDG performed the play successfully in their first invited dress rehearsal before an audience of 22. The second invited dress rehearsal was slightly marred by two very long and uncomfortable pauses in the middle of the play, during which none of the actors could think of what to say or do next. Someone had forgotten a line, and since the cast's concentration was not properly focused as it had been the night before, they were unable to recover as gracefully as one would have wished. Their experience is a common occurrence. Frequently, the first performance before an audience goes quite well. The actors are nervous and quite alert. Then the second performance, all too frequently, is a disappointment, usually due to the fact that the actors become overconfident and too relaxed. They forget that the previous evening's performance was the result of a certain amount of fear and a lot of presence of mind. The ISDG learned in a slightly uncomfortable situation that the director was not going to save them during the course of a performance. Once the play begins, the actors are on their own. Luckily the ISDG learned this in a rehearsal. Mistakes are allowed to happen there; after all, *that's what rehearsals are for!* The discomfort of the ISDG in dress rehearsal taught them something about performing which I am sure was a great contribution to their success during the official public performances.

The folly of many amateur productions is that after the company works for weeks or months on a play, the whole experience ends abruptly with one or two performances. Without invited audiences to practice in front of, the actors do all their stumbling in front of the very audience they have been working for weeks to please.

The more performances the cast goes through, the better. The last developmental stages a production goes through can occur only in performance. The show is not finished until the actors have the opportunity to make discoveries in performance and assimilate them. A play that is performed only once or twice is sure to feel unfinished.

The chance to perform a play more than once or twice gives amateur actors a chance to feel more in control as they learn to minimize "performance" errors. They learn to view errors as challenges—artistic problems needing artistic solutions—which can be worked out. The actors feel themselves grow as performers.

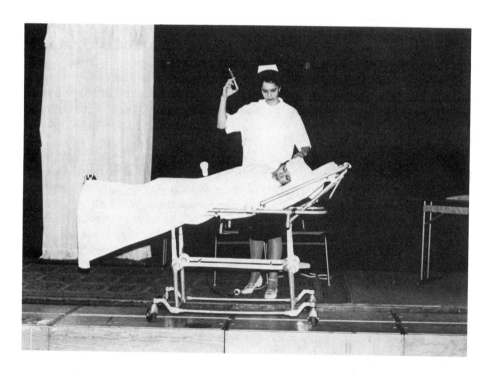

Last Rehearsals, *The Patient*: Props, costumes, and set pieces are added in the last few weeks of rehearsals. Having developed individual roles and a group interpretation of the story, the actors then work to project the story to the audience.

OPENING NIGHT

There is a great deal of psychology involved in pre-performance ritual. Actors and directors typically follow patterns that are established in the last few rehearsals and continue thorughout the run of the performances. This is another reason why the last few rehearsals should be considered performances.

Each night of the performance, the actors' rituals start while the actors are getting ready to come to the theater. They find themselves doing the same things each night. They are supposed to be at the theater at the same time each night, and each night they find that the pre-show preparation of the cast follows the same sequence, more or less. The actors greet their fellow company members, check the set and props, warm themselves up individually and with the cast, change into costumes and makeup, and then go backstage to wait for the show to begin. Every night the show begins with the same sounds and progresses in more or less the same way. All of this ritual is arranged by the director as a means of stabilizing the atmosphere for the actors. Each night, the actors find the familiar ritual an aid, which helps them make the transition from their daily selves to that of "the actor" and, eventually, "the character."

The ritual also provides a safety valve in the event that something does not happen according to schedule. If, for example, an actor is late, there is time for the stage manager to realize it and take steps to locate the person and bring him or her to the theater. If a can of red paint spills on a costume there is time and a controlled, relatively calm atmosphere in which to solve the problem. Problems that are not discovered and solved in the calm atmosphere of the pre-show could manifest themselves during the performance.

The director can add a positive "electricity" to the opening night as well. Actors need to be alert. The warm-up and backstage atmosphere should be charged with excitement, not panic, and the actors should be busy every minute. They should be taught to run their lines quietly in their heads backstage while waiting for the show to begin. During the show, when offstage, they may want to do the same, but they must also be alert to what is happening onstage so that they do not miss an entrance. On or offstage, concentration is crucial, and the director should make this point clear to the actors.

The behavior of the director on performance nights is much like that of an athletic coach before a game—positive mental attitude is essential. Spolin (1963) warns against a director transmitting his or her own stage fright to the actors. The actors, especially amateurs, need the director's support.

Supporting Roles

The Stage Manager

Every director needs a reliable stage manager. The stage manager should begin coming to rehearsals for the last two weeks, if not earlier. The stage manager's job is to preside over the backstage and stage areas during dress rehearsals and performances. The stage manager is the boss backstage, superior to the actors and crew. He or she signals the beginning of the show and is responsible for seeing to it that the actors do their job, that is, that they are ready and able to enter and perform when the time comes. The stage manager also communicates with other members of the backstage crew in order to be sure everyone is ready before the show begins. Except for preparing the cast, the director's job is finished when the performance begins. The director should be free to sit in the audience and watch the performance, allowing the stage manager to manage the cast and crew.

The Crew

People will be needed to assist by running the lights and sound and by helping the actors with their costumes, makeup, and any last minute details. Crew positions are ideal for students wishing to take part but not wishing to perform. The number of rehearsals a crew member needs to attend depends on the jobs he or she must do. Often, crew members are not needed until the last two weeks of rehearsal.

A "house" crew needs to be assembled for opening night. So that the director will be free to warm-up and otherwise prepare the actors, someone else is needed to sell tickets, greet the audience, hand out programs, and deal with any problems that might arise in the lobby or house (the house is the area where the audience sits). It is the responsibility of the house crew to see to it that the audience is comfortable. The "atmosphere" that the audience encounters upon arriving at the theater will influence their attitude toward the performance. Therefore, the house crew can determine the success or failure of a performance.

Advertising

Since a play needs an audience, advertising is needed. The performance of *The Long Christmas Dinner* was announced in a variety of ways. Newspapers are a source of free advertisement. I called the local city newspaper and asked the features editor if he would like to do a story on a new theater group in town. He needed material for the upcoming Wednesday edition so we met and talked, and a long article with a picture was printed. This article appeared two weeks before performances began. One of the foreign students in the cast called the university's student newspaper and secured a second feature article, which appeared the day before opening night.

Talking to the press is an exciting exercise for any articulate language learner. Students can be sent individually or in groups to meet with reporters to talk about the play. They should be prepared to have their words misinterpreted and in some cases put into their mouths by the reporters who are often looking for quotes to put into their article. Caution your students that the reporters might write down anything they say and that they should make sure that they are clear and accurate in the interview. Being misinterpreted by the press, or even misquoted, is a hazard which even native speakers of a language are subject to, but the publicity that results from interviews makes it a worthwhile experience to "meet the press."

The best kind of coverage the press can give a play is the type of article mentioned above. These are called "advances." In many towns where the theater "critics" are not always professionals and often are uninformed in the areas they are writing about, it is best to give them information in the form of an interview, as opposed to waiting until they write a "review" of a performance which may not have a positive effect on the audience.

Professional theaters usually prepare a "press packet" that describes the group and the current production, complete with information about the cast, director, and performance dates. These press packets are sent to all the newspapers and radio and television stations in the area. Occasionally the press will announce the event at no charge if they have space.

We sent an advertisement to three television stations and the fine arts radio station. All of these stations broadcast, free of charge, announcements of events that are of interest to the community. The following announcement was aired on local television and radio stations.

> The International Student Drama Group, a performing theater group with actors from six different countries, will perform Thornton Wilder's *The Long Christmas Dinner* at The Channing-Murray Foundation in Urbana, Wednesday and Thursday, April 29 and 30, at 8 P.M. Tickets are $1.50.

The most expensive form of advertising that we used was our poster. Posters are a standard form of publicity for plays. One of the foreign actresses in the cast was an advertising major, so it made sense that she should design the poster. The posters were posted around town by the cast. We concentrated heavily on some specific target areas where we felt the posters were most likely to catch the eyes of interested people.

We also distributed a flyer to the mailbox of each language teacher on the day before we opened. We felt that language teachers and their students were likely to be among the most interested in this project.

We were fortunate that one member of the cast was the president of the international student club at the local community college. He gave a presentation at one of their regular weekly meetings and invited the group to attend the last Monday night rehearsal free of charge. His presentation included a handout and the video-taped scene from the play.

The Cost

The total financial outlay for *The Long Christmas Dinner* was $161.50. As the following budget indicates, ticket sales recovered all but $10.00 of this money.

Poster for *The Long Christmas Dinner*. Design by Yanitza Ramirez de Smith.

The International Student Drama Group

presents

THE LONG CHRISTMAS DINNER

by Thornton Wilder

directed by Stephen Smith

CAST
(in order of speaking)

Lucia - Roderick's wife . . . . Connie Ng
Mother Bayard - Roderick's mother . . . . . . Maria Teresa Velasquez
Roderick Bayard - first head of a new household . . . . Emir Demirsoy
Cousin Brandon - Roderick's cousin . . . . Jeff Hubbel
Charles - son of Roderick and Lucia . . . . .Hisham Khayat
Genevieve - daughter of Roderick and Lucia . . . . Maria Teresa Velasquez
Leonora - Charles' wife . . . . Yanitza Ramirez
Cousin Ermengarde - distant relative of the Bayards . . . . . Jenny Goran
Sam - son of Charles and Leonora . . . . Gerardo Gonzalez
Lucia - daughter of Charles and Leonora . . . . Connie Ng
Roderick II - son of Charles and Leonora . . . . Emir Demirsoy

Time: Perhaps the late 1800's to the 1950's, but the action represents a reoccurring cycle that never stops.

Place: The Midwestern United States, near the Mississippi River.

PRODUCTION STAFF

scene and lighting consultant . . . . Gordon Wescliff
graphics and poster design . . . . Yanitza Ramirez
costumes and properties . . . . the company
stage manager . . . . Margie Berns
running crew . . . . Kathleen Burke, Yumiko Okada, Gail Barta

SPECIAL THANKS

Channing-Murray Foundation, Doug Brown and the Division of English as a Second Language, Rick Orr and the Celebration Company, Lloyd White, Netta Gillespie, University Orthopedics, Nancy Works, Gayle Kremers-Smith.

The ISDG salutes its counterparts in other parts of the world. Stimulus for this production comes in part from ISDGs in Austria, West Germany, Japan, England, The Netherlands, Hawaii, and Chicago.

Program for *The Long Christmas Dinner.*

One hundred and one persons attended the two public performances for which $1.50 admission was charged.

$ 19.00   posters
    30.00   programs
    20.00   royalties
    12.00   scripts
    20.00   rental of performance space
     5.50   make-up
     3.00   phone call to Samuel French, Inc.
     1.50   paper cups for backstage
     5.00   tape for sound
     4.00   dry cleaning for borrowed costumes
     4.50   backstage supplies
     7.00   copy shop costs for schedules, notices, etc.
     3.00   tickets
    15.00   Christmas dinner for cast (some food was donated)
     6.00   props (wine glasses, Christmas decorations)
     1.00   postage
     5.00   film for "photo call" (photographic record of show)
   161.50   TOTAL

All prices have been rounded to the nearest $.50.

Ticket sales: 101 tickets sold × $1.50 = $151.50.

ticket sales $151.50
cost   161.50
Total Loss = $ 10.00

Encore

The experience of the ISDG was a success, not only in terms of the performances, but as an English teaching and learning experience. Voluntarily, the group attended play rehearsals more hours per week than required for any other "course." This commitment to the project is an indication of the value that the students placed on it. In addition, the comments of the students themselves indicated a unanimous agreement that this was, for them, a highly valued and worthwhile experience, which they felt helped them improve their ability to communicate in English. Constant improvement in the students' abilities to use the English language was evident as the cast solved the many language problems that stood in the way of the final performances of the play. The implementation of an international student drama group for foreign students is a practical endeavor requiring only resources that a typical university or school already possesses; the most expensive resource is time.

Recommended Reading
and
Classroom Materials

Books on Acting and Directing for the Theater.

1. Barker, Clive. 1977. *Theatre Games.* Eyre Methuen Ltd. London, England. A philosophical and practical examination of the mental and physical processes of acting and how actors learn.

2. Cohen, Robert, John Harrop. 1974. *Creative Play Direction.* Prentice-Hall, Inc. Englewood Cliffs, N.J. A good textbook for directors.

3. Hagen, Uta. 1973. *Respect for Acting.* Macmillan Publishing Co., Inc. N.Y. A widely read, inspiring, and informative actor's book on acting.

4. Hodge, Francis, 1971. *Play Directing: Analysis, Communication, and Style.* Prentice-Hall, Inc. Englewood Cliffs, N.J. A good textbook for directors.

5. Hodgson, John, Ernest Richards. 1974. *Improvisation.* Grove Press, Inc. N.Y. A practical book that explains how to use improvisation when directing groups in the theater and education.

6. Langley, Stephen. 1974. *Theatre Management.* Drama Book Specialists/Publishers. N.Y. A nuts and bolts book on theater management for professionals and amateurs.

7. Lessac, Arthur. 1967. *The Use and Training of the Human Voice.* DBS Publications, Inc. Drama Book Specialists, N.Y. A very technical, but practical book for students and teachers of voice training: good insight into the teaching of voice control, pronunciation, learning accents, etc.

8. McGaw, Charles. 1980. *Acting is Believing,* Holt, Rinehart, and Winston, N.Y. A textbook for actors and acting teachers.

9. Spolin, Viola. 1963. *Improvisation for the Theater.* N. Western University Press, Evanston, Illinois. Theory, methodology, and techniques for training actors; includes many exercises.

10. Stanislavski, Constantin. 1936. *An Actor Prepares.* Elizabeth R. Hapgood, New York Theater Arts Books, N.Y. Dated, but classic, essay on the art of acting. Widely read in the world of professional theater.

11. Stanislavski, Constantin. 1949. *Building a Character.* E. R. Hapgood, New York Theater Arts Books. N.Y. Dated, but classic, essay on the art of acting. Widely read in the world of professional theater.

Materials for Language Teaching

Scenes, Sketches, and Short Plays

1. Ayckbourn, Alan, *et al.* 1977. *Mixed Doubles.* Samuel French Ltd. London. Eighteen short sketches about marriage.

2. Dixey, James, Mario Rinvolucri. 1978. *Get Up and Do It! Sketch and Mime for E.F.L.* Longman Group Ltd. London.

3. Elkind, Samuel. 1972. *32 Scenes For Acting Practice.* Scott, Foresman and Company. Glenview, Illinois.

4. Handman, Wynn. 1978. *Modern American Scenes for Student Actors.* Bantam Books, N.Y.

5. Hines, Mary E. 1980. *Skits in English.* Regents Publishing Co., Inc. N.Y. Written for ESL/EFL.

6. Methold, Ken. 1981. *The Music Line and Other Short Plays.* Longman Group Ltd. Harlow, Essex, England. Written for ESL/EFL.

7. Pinter, Harold. 1978. *Complete Works: TWO,* and *Complete Works: THREE.* Random House, Inc. N.Y. Eleven and ten short plays and sketches, respectively.

8. Pinter, Harold. 1964. *The Lover.* Samuel French, Ltd. London. A short one-act play.

9. Ramsey, Gaynor. 1978. *Play Your Part.* Longman Group Ltd. London. Simulated discussions for role playing; written for ESL/EFL.

10. Richards, Stanley, (ed.) 1978. *Twenty One-Act Plays: An Anthology for Amateur Performing Groups.* Doubleday and Co., Inc., Garden City, N.Y. Includes "The Patient" by Agatha Christie.

11. Schulman, Michael, and Eva Mekler. (eds.) 1980. *Contemporary Scenes for Student Actors.* Penguin Books, N.Y.

12. Steffensen, James, (ed.) 1965. *Great Scenes from The World Theater.* Avon Books, N.Y.

13. Thurber, James. 1962. *A Thurber Carnival.* Samuel French Inc., N.Y. Includes "A Unicorn in the Garden" and other short sketches.

14. Wilder, Thornton, 1931. *The Long Christmas Dinner.* Samuel French Inc., N.Y.

15. Young, J. W. 1973. *Audition Scenes for Students.* Vol. 2. The Dramatic Publishing Co. Chicago, Illinois.

Catalogs of Plays:

1. Dramatists Play Service, Inc. *Complete Catalogue of Plays 1982:1983.* Write to: 440 Park Avenue South, N.Y., N.Y. 10016.

2. Samuel French Ltd. *The Guide to Selecting Plays for Performance. Part 2. One Act Plays and Revue Sketches for Mixed Casts.* 84th Edition. Write to: Samuel French Ltd. 26 Southampton St. Strand London WC2E 7JE. This catalog lists available plays and includes plot summaries, type of setting, and character descriptions (numbers, sex, and type).

Games and Exercises:

1. See above: Barker, Cohen and Harrop, Hodge, Hodgson, Lessac, McGaw, Hines, Ramsey, and Spolin.

2. Graham, Carolyn. 1978 and 1979. *Jazz Chants: Rhythms of American English for Students of English as a Second Language.*, and *Jazz Chants for Children: Rhythms of American English through Chants, Songs, and Poems.* Oxford University Press, N.Y.

3. Maley, Alan, Alan Duff. 1978. *Drama Techniques in Language Learning.* Cambridge University Press, N.Y. Exercises for the language classroom.

4. McCallum, George P. *101 Word Games.* Oxford University Press, N.Y.

5. Wright, Andrew, David Betteridge, and Michael Buckby. 1979. *Games for Language Learning.* Cambridge University Press, N.Y.

Books on Drama for Language Teaching

1. Holden, Susan. 1981. *Drama in Language Teaching.* Longman Group Ltd. Harlow, Essex, England.

2. Via, Richard A. 1976. *English in Three Acts.* The University Press of Hawaii.

References

Arden, John. *Sergeant Musgrave's Dance*. New York: Grove Press, 1960.

Christie, Agatha. "The Patient." *Twenty One-Act Plays: An Anthology for Amateur Performing Groups*. Stanley Richards, ed., 1963.

Copland, Aaron. *Music and Imagination*. Cambridge, Mass.: Harvard University Press, 1975.

DeBono, Edward. *The Use of Lateral Thinking*. New York: Penguin Books, 1967.

Gordon, Raymond L. *Living in Latin America: A case in cross-cultural communication*. National Textbook Co. Skokie, Illinois 1974.

Hagen, Uta. *Respect for Acting*. New York: MacMillan Publishing Co., 1973.

Hodge, Francis. *Play Directing: Analysis Communication and Style*. Englewood Cliffs, N.J.: Prentice-Hall, Inc., 1971.

Horwitz, Elaine and Michael Horwitz, "Bridging Individual Differences. Empathy and Communicative Competence." *Personalizing Foreign Language Instruction*. Renate Schutz, ed. Skokie, Illinois: National Textbook Co., 1977.

Krashen, Stephen. "The Monitor Model for Adult Second Language Performance." *Viewpoints on English as a Second Language*. M. Burt and H. Dulay, eds. New York: Regents Publishing Co., 1977.

Lacey, Robert. *The Kingdom*. London, England: Hutchinson Pub. Co., 1981.

McGaw, Charles. *Acting Is Believing*. 4th ed. New York: Holt, Rinehart & Winston, 1980.

Nemser, W. "Approximative Systems of Foreign Language Learners." *International Review of Applied Linguistics* 9. 1971.

Oller, John W. *Language Tests at School*. London: Longman Group Ltd., 1979.

Pinter, Harold. *Complete Works: Two*. New York: Grove Press, 1961.

Purcell, Edward and Suter, Richard, "Predictors of Pronunciation Accuracy: A Reexamination." *Language Learning*, Vol. 30, No. 2., 1981.

Rabe, David. *Streamers*. New York: Samuel French, Inc., 1977.

Savignon, Sandra. *Communicative Competence: An Experiment in Foreign Language Teaching*. Philadelphia, Pa.: The Center for Curriculum Development, Inc., 1972.

Savignon, Sandra J. Communicative Competence: *Theory and Classroom Practice Texts and Contexts in Second Language Learning*. Addison-Wesley Publishing Co., Reading, Mass. 1983.

Spolin, Viola. *Improvisation for the Theater*. Evanston, Illinois: Northwestern University Press, 1963.

Stanislavski, Constantin. *An Actor Prepares*. trans. Elizabeth R. Hapgood. New York: New York Theater Arts Books, 1936.

Stanislavski, C. *Building a Character*. trans. Elizabeth R. Hapgood. New York: New York Theater Arts Books, 1949.

Thurber, James. *A Thurber Carnival*. New York: Samuel French, Inc., 1962.

Weller, Michael. *Moonchildren*. New York: Samuel French, Inc., 1971.

Widdowson, H. G. *Explorations in Applied Linguistics*. Oxford: Oxford University Press, 1979.

Widdowson, H. G. "Interpretive Procedures and the Importance of Poetry." *Explorations in Applied Linguistics*. Oxford: Oxford University Press, 1979.

Wilder, Thornton. *The Long Christmas Dinner*. New York: Samuel French, Inc., 1934.

Wright, William Aldis. *The Complete Works of Shakespeare*. Garden City, New York: Doubleday & Co., Inc., 1936.

Index